What readers are about "Marriage by the Book"

"Doug Britton's 'Marriage by the Book' series is the most thoroughly biblical, deeply practical, and user-friendly marriage resource I have seen in thirty years of study and use. These books provide clarity, relevance, and biblicity for self-study, mentoring, or small group leadership, and are so well written that lay leaders can use them immediately without having to be experts. They will positively impact your marriage and the marriages of those you lead."
John Morrison, Family Life Pastor
Fellowship Bible Church, Winchester, Virginia

"'Marriage by the Book' is well written, engaging, and biblically-based, with numerous insights from Doug's years of counseling couples. I especially like the many practical, down-to-earth suggestions he offers. Get the series, do the study and exercises, and then watch what happens!"
Dann Bryant, Associate Pastor
Arcade Church, Sacramento, California

"I really appreciate the approach in *Laying a Solid Foundation*. It deals with foundational issues that help people behave like Christians! (So many books jump into big marriage issues without first laying the groundwork.) We've used this book in a small group Bible study and in counseling. 'Marriage by the Book' is the best marriage resource I've encountered."
David Dickinson, Senior Pastor
Hope Evangelical Free Church, Kearney, Nebraska

"'Marriage by the Book' is fantastic, easy to read and easy to understand. The books are highly relevant and practical, bringing the Scriptures alive. We love the format—it helps us lead as well as helps couples grasp the material."
Larry and Gloria Lara, Small Group Leaders
Yosemite Christian Center, Madera, California

"My pastor asked me to find the best marriage material for our small group marriage ministry. I liked 'Marriage by the Book' the most of every resource I reviewed. It is biblically-based and practical, reminding you of the simple things you don't think of every day (such as praying together daily as a couple). Our group has seen really positive results from applying these biblical truths."

Jeremy and Danielle Milligan, Small Group Leaders
Baptist Temple Church, Reidsville, North Carolina

"When our Life Group studied 'Laying a Solid Foundation,' the couples really appreciated its practical application questions and the way it prompted open sharing in the group. Everyone was sad when the study came to an end. Even though we were the leaders and already had a strong marriage, this book helped us a lot too!"

Jef and Shannon Klein, Life Group Leaders
Coastal Life Christian Church, Coronado, California

"What's the greatest gift a couple can give its children? The example of a great marriage. I have seen numerous marriages improve by leaps and bounds as people studied 'Marriage by the Book'! I love its Bible-based step-by-step approach to making giant changes. I highly recommend these practical books, as well as all of Doug Britton's books."

Earl Radford, Board Member and Children's Pastor
International Network of Children's Ministries

"'Marriage by the Book' is a wonderful tool to help even the best of marriages become better. Many times it feels as if Doug has been sitting in our home as we have dealt with the issues he addresses. Every married couple should go through this series at least once. We have been married over 35 years, and the last two years since we have been involved with 'Marriage by the Book' have been the best by far ... and they are just getting better."

Bob and April Basura, Small Group Leaders
Capital Christian Center, Sacramento, California

MARRIAGE BY THE BOOK

Book 1

Laying a Solid Foundation

for
Couples
Individuals
Small groups
Marriage classes

Practical • Biblical • Cross-cultural

Doug Britton, MFT

LifeTree Books
Sacramento, California

"Marriage by the Book" was first published in 1993 as a single volume titled "Keys to a Great Marriage." It was renamed February 1997 as "Marriage by the Book." Later that year it was expanded into an eight-book series titled "Marriage by the Book." The eight books in this series were updated in 2010.

The stories in this book are true, although names and identifying details have been changed to maintain confidentiality.

MBBMC120100114S

ISBN 978-1-930153-01-1

Printed in the United States of America

Published by LifeTree Books
Sacramento, Calif.
www.LifeTreeBooks.com

I want to express my deep appreciation to my sons Zach and Josh, their wives Holly and Paige, and the hundreds of couples and small groups that have offered invaluable suggestions after studying the "Marriage by the Book" series. This book, and all the books in the series, are in a large part the result of your help.

Most of all, I am deeply grateful to my wife Skeeter for her countless insightful comments, painstaking editing, prayers, and love.

•

Now to him who is able to do immeasurably more than all we ask or imagine, according to his power that is at work within us, to him be glory in the church and in Christ Jesus throughout all generations, for ever and ever! Amen. (Ephesians 3:20-21)

BOOKS BY DOUG BRITTON

Books for Daily Living
Breaking Free from Alcohol and Drugs
Conquering Depression
Defeating Temptation
Healing Life's Hurts
How to Lead a Christ-Centered Small Group
Overcoming Jealousy and Insecurity
Strengthening Your Marriage
Successful Christian Parenting
Victory Over Grumpiness, Irritation, and Anger
Who Do You Think You Are?

Marriage by the Book (eight-book series)
Laying a Solid Foundation
Making Christ the Cornerstone
Encouraging Your Spouse
Extending Grace to Your Mate
Talking with Respect and Love
Improving Your Teamwork
Putting Money in its Place
Fanning the Flames of Romance
Marriage by the Book Group Leaders' Guide

BOOKS BY DOUG BRITTON

Books for growing in Christ (a discipleship series)

Getting Connected

First Things First

Hand In Hand

Twenty-eight Days

To see a current list of books by Doug Britton, MFT, visit:

www.DougBrittonBooks.com

Contents

Foreword

Skeeter and I were university students when we learned she was pregnant. She was nineteen, I was twenty, and we were not married. We were not at all pleased with this turn of events.

We decided to get married, but shortly after the wedding we were so miserable we almost had an abortion. Instead, we had our son Zach, the first of three.

Our marriage started poorly and went downhill from there. We separated, got back together, and then continued going downhill. We were headed for divorce when, about three years later, we became Christians. God dramatically reversed our direction and we began to learn how to love each other. This book draws from our story and the stories of many couples I have counseled over the years, couples who have overcome every sort of difficulty to make good lives together.

Most marriages start out better than ours did, with two people who are certain they can craft a wonderful union. After all, they are in love, aren't they? Yet as the years go by, many never experience the passionate, joyful life they expected.

Why not? After seeing God rebuild our relationship, and after helping thousands of families as a counselor, seminar speaker and Bible teacher, one reason stands out: Many do not know the Bible's instructions for *how* to create a great marriage. Thousands of years ago one of God's prophets said, *"My people are destroyed from lack of knowledge" (Hosea 4:6)*. That statement is true of marriages today.

Are all marriages in trouble? Of course not, but they all are works in progress. You may be reading this book for a minor tune-up or to help a good marriage get better. On the other hand, you may need a major overhaul. Whatever your situation, you will find practical information that will help.

As you study, you will read the stories of many couples I have counseled. Even if it's hard to imagine going through trials like theirs, don't discount the lessons their stories illustrate. Not only will their experiences help you in your day-to-day life, they also will prepare you for troubles you may face down the road.

If you are in the midst of great difficulties, let me offer encouragement. Again and again I have seen marriages that seemed impossibly damaged become vital and happy with God's help. Regardless of your situation, there is hope—the sure hope that comes from God and the truth of his Word, the Bible.

May God bless you as you read. And may he help you build a marriage that is rich and rewarding, comfortable and exhilarating, tenderhearted and enduring.

Doug Britton

Introduction

We live in an age of countless and ever-changing opinions and theories about marriage. When we seek guidance, it is hard to know whom to believe.

Yet there is a dependable source to which we can go, one proven trustworthy and constant throughout history—the Word of God.

 All Scripture is God-breathed and is useful for teaching, rebuking, correcting and training in righteousness, so that the man of God may be thoroughly equipped for every good work. (2 Timothy 3:16-17)

The Bible covers it all, including communication, forgiveness, decision-making, finances, and making love. God invented marriage. He knows how to make it work.

Laying a Solid Foundation takes ageless truths from the Bible and helps you apply them in your marriage. It is part of an eight-book series called "Marriage by the Book." Although it stands as a complete book by itself, I encourage you also to read the other seven books since they build on one another, each presenting the Bible's teaching on a different aspect of marriage. The eight books are:

1. *Laying a Solid Foundation*

2. *Making Christ the Cornerstone*

3. *Encouraging Your Spouse*

4. *Extending Grace to Your Mate*

5. *Talking with Respect and Love*

    6. *Improving Your Teamwork*

    7. *Putting Money in its Place*

    8. *Fanning the Flames of Romance*

Books are designed for individual or group study.
The books are designed to be studied by an individual, a couple, a small group, or a marriage class. They also can be assigned as homework by a pastor, counselor, or mentor. Although written for married people, these books are excellent pre-marriage resources.

Small group guidelines are at the back of this book.
Each book has six chapters, making it convenient for a six-week small group study. The "Guidelines for Small Group Leaders" at the back of this book show how to structure meetings and lead a group. These guidelines include suggested chapter-by-chapter discussion questions.

A separate book with more extensive guidelines, the *Marriage by the Book Group Leaders' Guide,* also is available. It includes step-by-step procedures for churches starting a marriage ministry, suggestions for handling typical small group problems, and much more.

Each person should have his or her own book.
Many "Make it personal" questions with spaces for answers are scattered throughout this book. If you are studying as a couple, each person should have a book so both husband and wife can write answers and comments.

Names have been changed.
As you read, you will see that I have drawn upon the experiences of people I have counseled. The stories are true, but names and identifying details have been changed to maintain confidentiality.

Turn to the Source of Truth

God's Word, the Bible, tells us that God wants to help you become the best man or woman, and best husband or wife, you can be. When you turn to him, he is available to help you in practical, concrete ways. The question is, how can we get close to God?

As I grew up, I could see that something was drastically wrong with almost everyone I knew. I rarely saw the quality of love and trust between people that I felt should be there. I did not observe this lack in others only. I knew that something was missing in me.

I explored different philosophies, schools of psychology, sociological approaches, metaphysical ideas, and religions. Many sounded reasonable at first, but as I evaluated their reality in my life and in the lives of those who embraced them, they seemed hollow.

I thought there was a spiritual element to life, but couldn't figure out what it was. But God drew both Skeeter and me to him. Following a series of unexpected events, we surrendered our lives to Jesus Christ and were "born again" (John 3:3-7).

As I grew in my Christian walk, I learned about original sin, the sin of Adam and Eve that cripples us all. Here, finally, was an explanation that rang true, a reason for the "something wrong" I had observed and experienced. To my delight, I finally began to see this "something wrong" in me changing for the better. I still have a long way to go, but I am thankful for the work God has done so far.

Jesus offers each of us a walk with God and a fullness of life that is not possible without him. He said, *"I tell you the truth, no one can see the kingdom of God unless he is born again" (John 3:3).* He also said, *"I am the bread of life" (John 6:35),* and *"I am the way and the truth and the life. No one comes to the Father except through me" (John 14:6).*

When we come to God "through Jesus," we are "born again." We become Christians—followers of Christ.

How does one become a Christian? Paul wrote:

If you confess with your mouth, "Jesus is Lord," and believe in your heart that God raised him from the dead, you will be saved. For it is with your heart that you believe and are justified, and it is with your mouth that you confess and are saved. (Romans 10:9-10)

"Believe" means to "adhere to, trust in, and rely on the truth" (Amplified Bible). Becoming a Christian is not simply joining a church or acting religious. It is surrendering your life to Christ and allowing his Spirit to dwell within you.

Do not assume you are a Christian because of your background or church membership. Being raised by Christians does not automatically make you a Christian, nor does going to church, seeking to live a moral life, serving as an elder, or leading as a pastor. What counts is whether you have given your life to Jesus Christ.

If you have never done so, I invite you to present yourself to him now, for *"everyone who calls on the name of the Lord will be saved" (Romans 10:13)*. Surrender your life to God by accepting Jesus as your Savior and Lord. Then allow God to begin the process of transforming you into the best man or woman, and best husband or wife, you can be.

Make it personal ____ ✐

Have you surrendered your life to Christ? If not, read the following as a prayer:

"Dear Lord, I confess that I am a sinner. Please forgive my sins and accept me as your child. I invite you to be my Savior and the Lord of my life. I surrender myself to you in the name of Jesus Christ."

If you prayed with sincerity, Christ accepted you into his Kingdom, and you are now a Christian. Welcome to the family of God!

I accepted Jesus Christ as my Savior and Lord today. Thank you, Jesus!

_____   _____
Signature   Date

Not only will God help your marriage, he will transform your life. You have an exciting life ahead of you. These four suggestions will help you get started in your Christian walk:

- Tell someone that you accepted Christ.
- Read the Bible daily, starting in the New Testament with the Gospel of John.
- Join a Bible-believing church.
- Pray regularly.

Getting the Most from this Book

*Do your best to present yourself to God as one approved,
a workman who does not need to be ashamed and who
correctly handles the word of truth. (2 Timothy 2:15)*

By reading this book, you are demonstrating a desire for a more fulfilling marriage. The following guidelines will help you accomplish your goal. They are based on the experiences of hundreds of people who studied an earlier version. If you follow these suggestions, they will help you reach your goal more quickly, efficiently, and gracefully.

Pray for God's help.

Changing is hard work. In fact, many think change is impossible after a child is only a few years old. Yet with God, nothing is impossible (Luke 1:37). When we turn to him, we discover he provides *"incomparably great power for us who believe" (Ephesians 1:19).*

As you read, ask God to help you learn and apply each lesson. When you come across a challenging guideline, do not say, "That's not the kind of person I am," or, "I wasn't raised that way." Instead, pray for a teachable attitude. As you draw near to God, he will draw near to you (James 4:8).

Some of the "Make it personal" sections in this book suggest you write prayers asking God's help. Write them, and then go back and pray them every few days.

Other "Make it personal" sections include printed prayers. When you get to them, either read them as prayers or say your own prayers to the Lord.

Make it personal ___

Write a short prayer asking God's help as you study this book.

Go to the Bible.
Do not be governed by your emotions. Instead, be ruled by the Word of God. It is the Lord's instruction book and more, for God dwells in his Word.

As you study, go to the source. Look up every Scripture. Meditate on key verses throughout the day. Memorize the verses in "Putting It All Together" at the end of each chapter.

> *For the word of God is living and active. Sharper than any double-edged sword, it penetrates even to dividing soul and spirit, joints and marrow; it judges the thoughts and attitudes of the heart. (Hebrews 4:12)*

Read this book to learn *how to love* your spouse.
People often read marriage books to find ammunition that supports their case in ongoing arguments. I urge you not to do

this. Instead, look for ways to better love your husband or wife. Approach each chapter with the attitude of, "What can I learn today? How can I apply it?"

Jesus said the second most important commandment, right after loving God, is to love your neighbor as yourself (Mark 12:31). Learn to love your spouse as your closest neighbor.

Focus on changes you, personally, should make.

Most of us focus on our spouse's faults. Yet Jesus said, *"First take the plank out of your own eye" (Matthew 7:5)*. As you read, focus on changes *you* should make, not on those you wish your spouse would make.

Study even if your spouse does not.

I hope you and your mate will study and learn together, but your spouse may refuse. In fact, he or she may say, "I don't have any problems. You're the one who needs help. Study by yourself."

What could be more frustrating? After all, your mate has problems. Everyone does. You know it, and God knows it. But your spouse doesn't seem to know it.

However, even if your mate refuses to study, work through this book yourself. Don't say, "I'll read it, but only if you will." Instead, learn how to be the best husband or wife possible. God can perform miracles in your personal life—and in your marriage—as you study.

Discipline yourself to follow a study plan.

Do not look for a quick fix. Set up regular times to study, and then discipline yourself to follow your plan. If necessary, ask your spouse or a friend to hold you accountable for following through.

Do not read too many pages at one sitting. Study one or two chapters each week and then pray about, meditate on, and practice what you learned.

Learn all the principles.

Each chapter presents biblical truths. Do not take them lightly, choosing what you like and discarding those things that are personally challenging. Learn everything God has to say about marriage.

Write an answer to each question.

This book is designed to be interactive, with numerous "Make it personal" questions throughout to help you apply the material to your life. Think about each question and write your answer. In addition, underline key points as you read. Write notes in the margins or a notebook.

If you find it difficult to write answers, I encourage you to overcome your reluctance or embarrassment. The more you involve yourself by answering the questions, the more the information will become part of you and the more you will change.

Practice what you learn.

Don't read about God's principles without putting them into practice. That would be like going to a doctor but refusing to take your medicine, or studying nutrition but refusing to eat healthy food. Paul wrote, *"Whatever you have learned or received or heard from me, or seen in me—put it into practice"* *(Philippians 4:9)*.

James illustrated the same truth when he wrote, *"Do not merely listen to the word, and so deceive yourselves. Do what it says" (James 1:22)*. Look at the principles you learn as bricks in a wall. The more secure the first bricks, the stronger the wall.

Review each chapter from time to time to be sure you don't forget key principles. In addition, make a list of points that particularly apply to your life. This will help you avoid slipping back into old habits and having to learn the same lessons all over again.

Be appreciative if your spouse makes an effort.

Do not feel insulted if your mate follows some of the suggestions in these books. For example, if he or she asks you out to dinner, don't say, "You're just asking because you're supposed to." Or if your spouse apologizes for something, resist the temptation to respond, "You don't really mean it. You're only saying that because you know you're supposed to apologize."

The point of this book is to help people change. Be appreciative when your spouse makes an effort.

Continue to apply this material over your lifetime.

As your marriage improves, you may be tempted to shift into cruise control. Don't make this mistake! Becoming complacent is a sure-fire way to slide back into old habits. Continue to throw yourself into your relationship throughout your life. Keep practicing what you have learned.

Think of your marriage as a young tree planted in a park. It may not be much to look at now, but it is full of promise. Water, fertilize, and prune it. After years it will fill the sky, giving shade and peace to generations. Never stop tending it.

Make it personal ＿＿ ✎

Name two of these guidelines that will help you as you study. Describe why they will be helpful.

(1)

(2)

Be Patient

You may find yourself becoming frustrated that you or your spouse are not progressing as fast as you would like. Take inspiration from the book of Hebrews. Although we are told not to be lazy, we also are told to be patient.

 We do not want you to become lazy, but to imitate those who through faith and patience inherit what has been promised. (Hebrews 6:12)

Give yourself time to change.
You may be able to read this book in a matter of hours, but you could never put it into practice that quickly. That would be like reading a book on skiing and then launching yourself from the top of the steepest ski slope, thinking you could race downhill like a professional.

If you do not need to make lots of major changes, count yourself fortunate. On the other hand, if you face many challenges, do not be impatient. You and your spouse may have experienced a lifetime of pain. It may have taken years for your problems to develop. Do not expect them to go away overnight.

God performs miracles, but growth is usually a slow process. Be patient with yourself and with your spouse. It takes time to change old habits.

Do not be overwhelmed by the information.
You may become discouraged by the many suggestions in this book, thinking you cannot follow them all. Don't feel condemned and do not try to do everything at once. There is a lot of material.

At the end of each chapter, "Putting It All Together" provides a place to identify one or two things you want to work on the most. That should be enough for starters. Come back to the chapter later for fine-tuning.

Recognize improvements.

Some time ago, I counseled Frank and Janet and gave them a homework assignment of praying together twice each day. Both enthusiastically agreed.

When we met again one week later, Janet was hurt, frustrated and angry because Frank had only prayed with her on two days. She thought this proved he did not love her.

Frank should have followed through on his commitment and needed to apologize. But Janet needed to recognize and appreciate the improvement. Praying together two days in one week was more than they ever had done before.

Do not be discouraged if new problems come up.

As you read, you may become aware of problems that you had not noticed before. Don't be discouraged. Instead, look at this as something positive. Think of it as taking your car in for an oil change only to have the mechanic point out a leak in the radiator. By taking care of it now, you will avoid serious problems down the road.

Do not give up when there are setbacks.

Here is a pattern I see over and over: A couple experiences great improvements, then old problems reappear, and one of them says, "I guess we haven't changed. I give up."

When this happens, don't give up. All marriages suffer reverses and difficult moments from time to time. Expect them, learn from them, and press on.

Make it personal ___ 🖎

How will the above suggestions help you be patient?

Invite Your Mate to Study with You

I encourage you and your spouse to study this book together. Talking about these lessons can be exciting, even life-changing. Yet such discussions can degenerate into accusations, name-calling, anger, and hurt feelings. The following guidelines will help you avoid common problems and get the most out of your time together.

Invite (but don't pressure) your mate.

Let your spouse know you would enjoy studying together, but don't start a fight over it. If your mate says "no," don't get into an argument. Instead, study alone.

Set up a regular time to talk.

Do not simply say, "We need to talk about this book sometime." Make specific plans. Agree on a schedule. For example, you could study together at any of these times:

- Fifteen minutes every night after dinner

- 7:00 to 7:30 p.m. Monday and Friday nights

- 9:00 to 10:00 a.m. every Saturday

Decide if you want to read separately before talking.

Some couples like to read a chapter separately and then get together to discuss it. Others prefer to read together and talk about the material as they go. Still others do both, reading when apart and then when together.

Start with prayer.

Invite God to play a central part in your discussion. Ask him to:

- Show each of you what you need to work on the most.

- Give you grace and discipline to change.

- Help you talk with love and respect.

Read a few paragraphs, and then discuss them.

A common pattern for those who study together is for one person to read a few paragraphs out loud, after which both discuss the material. The second person then reads, followed again by a brief discussion. This process is often repeated for twenty or thirty minutes.

Don't worry if you find a point that is especially relevant and spend the entire time focusing on it. The idea is to deal with real issues, not just turn pages.

When you review the "Make it personal" questions, each can read his or her written answers or just share verbally.

Get involved.

Do not simply say, "I agree with that." Go into detail. Explain why you think what you do.

Share *personal* insights when you talk.

Talk about how the material applies to you, personally. Instead of pointing out what you think your mate should learn, discuss changes *you* should make.

Don't get mad at your mate's comments.

If you tell each other your answers to "Make it personal" questions, sometimes you may be hurt by things your spouse says. Ask God to help you avoid reacting in anger or self-pity. There may be things you can learn from your mate's answers. Ask the Lord to help you respond with wisdom, understanding, and love.

Write your own answer to each question.

Do not ask your mate to write answers for both of you. Write your own answers.

Ask before reading what your spouse wrote.

Your spouse may write thoughts, fears or temptations he or she desires to keep private. Agree not to read each other's answers without permission. As I wrote before, each person should have his or her own book if possible. Otherwise, think about writing your answers in separate notebooks to maintain privacy.

Make it personal ___ 🖉

If you and your spouse plan to discuss this book together, write the day(s) and time(s) you will talk.

Putting It All Together — Getting the Most from this Book

Key point: Ask God to help you have the attitude of a learner as you study this book.

Memory verse: *"Do your best to present yourself to God as one approved, a workman who does not need to be ashamed and who correctly handles the word of truth." (2 Timothy 2:15)*

Action plan: Choose one or two lessons from "Getting the Most from this Book" you will work on this week:

1.

2.

Chapter 1

Realize You are "One Flesh"

*"The two will become one flesh." So they are no longer
two, but one. (Mark 10:8)*

G od saw that it was not good for Adam to live alone, so he
created Eve (Genesis 2:18-22). He intended marriage to
be the most intimate of human relationships, an answer to
the profound loneliness in Adam's heart.

God's definition of marriage, which sets it apart from all
other relationships, is that a man and a woman become *"one
flesh" (Genesis 2:24)*. You are one flesh if you have a great
marriage. You also are one flesh if you have a rotten marriage, were not a Christian when you married, or think you
married the wrong person.

*The man said, "This is now bone of my
bones and flesh of my flesh; she shall be called
'woman,' for she was taken out of man." For
this reason a man will leave his father and
mother and be united to his wife, and they will
become one flesh. (Genesis 2:23-24)*

*Has not the LORD made them one? In flesh
and spirit they are his. (Malachi 2:15)*

You cannot get any closer to another person than being
one flesh. On the other hand, although you are one flesh, each
of you also is a separate and complete individual. The two are
one, and the one is two.

Since we are one flesh, everything I do to my wife Skeeter,
I do to myself. When I hurt her, I harm myself. When I am

kind to her, I am blessed. Paul made this point when he wrote, *"In this same way, husbands ought to love their wives as their own bodies. He who loves his wife loves himself"* *(Ephesians 5:28)*. This principle also applies to wives loving their husbands.

Some rewards of a healthy marriage are:

- **Intimacy**

    A marriage can soar to heights of love denied all other human relationships. Couples can experience unparalleled spiritual, emotional, intellectual, and sexual bonds. To begin to grasp the possibilities of marital intimacy, read the Song of Songs. Passionate verses toward the end summarize Solomon's message:

> *Love ... burns like blazing fire, like a mighty flame. Many waters cannot quench love; rivers cannot wash it away. If one were to give all the wealth of his house for love, it would be utterly scorned. (Song of Songs 8:6-7)*

    Intimacy can also be experienced in small ways: a tender goodbye kiss, laughter over a corny joke, or a love note. Intimacy in marriage is both exciting and comfortable.

- **Teamwork and mutual support**

    Two people united can do much more than two apart. God said that husband and wife, *together,* would rule over the earth (Genesis 1:27-28). Each can encourage, praise, and build up the other. When one is weak, the other can be strong.

    In addition, we can learn from one another since each has different strengths, personalities and skills. For instance, I learned much from Skeeter about the nurturing side of parenting, while she learned how to calmly discipline our children from me.

Two are better than one, because they have a good return for their work: If one falls down, his friend can help him up. But pity the man who falls and has no one to help him up! (Ecclesiastes 4:9-10)

Just as a sports team profits from players with different skills, so you and your spouse can profit from the different abilities you bring to your marriage. Being different from each other means you have more gifts, interests, and talents collectively than either of you has individually.

- **Children**

    Although children are not necessary for a happy marriage, many of us have discovered bringing up children to be one of life's greatest joys. As Skeeter and I think about our years together, we see few blessings that match the privilege of raising three sons.

 God blessed them and said to them, "Be fruitful and increase in number." (Genesis 1:28)

Sons are a heritage from the LORD, children a reward from him. (Psalm 127:3)

Make it personal ___ ✐

What does the Bible mean by "one flesh"?

What are some things you do well as a team? (If you can't think of any, don't give up. By the time you finish the "Marriage by the Book" series, you will be able to list many things.)

Identify Reasons for Problems

Some people have a great time being married and enjoy their one flesh relationship. Others constantly fight, while others coexist as roommates. Still others live like hostile cellmates. Divorce abounds.

Some common reasons for marriage problems are listed below. Whether your marriage is soaring to the heights or plunging to the depths, you probably will see at least one or two points that describe you. By checking each one that applies to you, you can become aware of things to focus on as you study this book.

When We Married

☐ **I did not know biblical marriage principles.**

Many of us have little or no understanding of the scriptural principles that we need to follow to build a good marriage. We are like someone who tries to fly an airplane by randomly pushing buttons and pulling levers instead of learning how to do it.

You may have watched pilots in action at the movies or flown thousands of miles as a passenger, yet if you try to fly a plane, it probably won't get off the ground. If it does, it most likely will have a bumpy flight and a crash landing.

Marriage was once like that for Skeeter and me. We talked late into the night again and again, seeking to get close, trying to figure out what marriage was all about. We separated for a few months, then got back together and moved far from everyone we knew, determined to start afresh.

Once again, we talked and talked late into the night, yet the rift between us grew. Advice from those around us was of little help since they too did not know biblical principles. We were headed toward divorce before we turned to Christ and found the help we needed.

We finally discovered what countless others found before us: Creating a great marriage is an even more mysterious and complex task than flying a plane. We need instructions from the manufacturer's handbook—the Bible.

☐ **I married while blinded by romantic love.**

God has given us the capacity to love passionately. It is a wonderful gift, yet it can be deceptive.

Many are so swept up by their emotions that they marry without getting to know the other person beyond a superficial level. They do not pray for God's guidance, talk with their pastor, or ask the advice of parents or friends. They ignore danger signals, certain their love will overcome all difficulties. When problems arise after the wedding, they feel confused or betrayed.

☐ **I had unrealistic expectations.**

Many marry with unrealistic expectations. For example, if your mother waited on your father as a serving woman would wait on a king, you might have thought your wife would do the same.

Perhaps your expectations were of a more spiritual nature. You read dozens of Christian marriage books and thought your spouse would be like the sensitive and loving people described in the books. Then you awoke to find yourself married to someone consumed by a job or addicted to television.

If you were particularly unrealistic, you may have married a verbally or physically abusive person, hoping the anger would go away once you married. Instead, when you became husband and wife, your spouse's anger grew.

☐ **I was unaware of my spouse's expectations.**

Many of us think we know each other well before marrying. Once married, we are surprised at our spouse's hidden expectations. For example, you may have been shocked to learn that your wife assumes you will cook half the meals, take out the garbage, change jobs, and stop hanging out with your buddies. Or you may have been astonished to learn that your husband expects you to help earn a living, mow the lawn, wash his clothes, and clean up his messes.

☐ **I felt pressured to be married.**

Some reluctantly marry because others tell them it is God's will. Others, such as Skeeter and myself, marry because of pregnancy. Still others marry because of guilt over sexual activities. If you married primarily because of pressure from your spouse-to-be or others, you are likely to experience regret and resentment.

☐ **I brought pain from a former marriage.**

Previous relationships can affect the way you respond to your husband or wife. If a former spouse was unfaithful, you may overreact when your current mate comes home thirty minutes late. If your previous husband or wife was abusive, you may cringe at any hint of anger in your present spouse.

☐ **I didn't know marriage takes so much work.**
    You may have stopped working on your relationship
after the wedding, thinking that once married, you could
take it easy and enjoy the ride. Then when the ride turned
bumpy, you became bitter. You may have decided that you
married the wrong person, or that you and your spouse
have "grown apart."
    But the real problem may have been your expectation
of automatic happiness. Good marriages do not just happen. They require attention and effort.
    In general, men seem less aware of this than women.
Some do what comes easiest, not putting thought or special effort into developing their marriage. "I earn a decent
living, don't fool around with other women, and stay so-
ber," they say. "What more could any woman want?"

Make it personal ___ ✐

Describe any of the above factors that were true for you when
you married. If you have overcome any of them, what made the
difference?

Describe other events from your past that have negatively affected your marriage (such as someone's bad example, childhood trauma, or rape).

_____

Since We Married

☐ **My job is draining me.**
Society oversells both men and women on the importance of a career. We try to find fulfillment in our jobs and neglect our families. Countless people have looked back at the end of their lives and deeply regretted such misplaced priorities.

☐ **I am consumed by home tasks.**
Some spend so much time decorating their home, cleaning, entertaining friends, gardening, remodeling, or working on the yard that they neglect their spouse.

☐ **I am a nag.**
You may continually complain because you are disappointed and frustrated with your spouse or other aspects of your life.

☐ **I am repeating my parents' bad habits.**

Maybe your parents screamed at each other. Or they may have scarcely spoken to each other, harboring grudges and self-pity. Whatever their patterns, you may imitate them without realizing it, bringing their pain into your marriage. We often imitate what we have seen, even if we hated it.

If your father rarely spoke to your mother, you may have been upset to learn that your wife wants to talk all the time. You were willing to talk while courting, when things were new and exciting. But you never imagined that marriage would require ongoing communication at a deeper level than, "What's for dinner?"

Or perhaps your mother talked to your father as if he were a little boy. If she did, there is a good chance that you have slipped into the same way of talking to your husband.

☐ **I am casual about sexual immorality.**

People all around us consider sexual immorality to be normal and acceptable. This is true in media, entertainment, and society at large. In many TV shows and movies, unmarried people are sexually active and married people have affairs. This is treated as normal, or even desirable. Internet sites, magazines, detective books, romance books, and other novels routinely describe immoral sexual activity in a positive light.

Even our news media frequently portray the adulteries of married people and the sexual affairs of single people as fun and entertaining. In essence, many segments of our society have given a big thumbs up to sexual immorality.

This casual approach to sex has resulted in devastating damage to innumerable marriages. Countless people have harbored secret lusts, flirted with others, or engaged in sexual sins and discovered that these activities are not harmless after all.

☐ **I focus on "meeting my own needs."**
Many people think that "meeting our own needs" should be our first priority. Instead of serving our spouse, we focus on our own desires.

☐ **Sometimes I say we should divorce.**
Although God said, *"I hate divorce" (Malachi 2:16),* divorce for non-biblical reasons is socially acceptable to many. There often is little expectation, even within much of the Christian community, that a couple will work through their problems and rebuild a marriage.

☐ **I have an unbalanced view of "headship."**
Some men believe that all the Bible has to say about marriage is that the wife must submit to the husband. Such a man may say, "The real problem in our marriage is that she won't obey me." This attitude demonstrates little understanding of God's instructions about "servant leadership," or the husband's responsibility to love his wife.

On the other hand, some women are afraid to think or act without their husband's permission. They have not heeded the example of the powerful, productive woman described in Proverbs 31:10-31.

Other women go to the opposite extreme, entirely rejecting the principle of the husband's leadership. They are unaware of the many Scriptures that deal with this subject, or they choose to ignore them as old-fashioned and not relevant for today.

Make it personal ___ 🖉

Describe any of the above problems that apply to you.

If some of the above problems applied in the past, but no longer do, what made the difference? How has the change improved your marriage?

Describe other problems that have negatively affected your marriage (such as drug or alcohol abuse, financial pressures, children, stepchildren, getting in a rut, illness, or lukewarm Christianity).

Look at the Positive

Whew! Although going through the previous pages can be enlightening, it also can be unpleasant. Let's take a few minutes to look at some more cheerful things.

Identify positive influences.

One of the best ways to learn is by example. Paul wrote to the Corinthians, *"Follow my example, as I follow the example of Christ" (1 Corinthians 11:1).* Maybe your parents provided you with a good example of marriage. Perhaps their marriage was not successful overall, yet still offers some good ideas. Or perhaps you have to look a little farther for positive examples—to your pastor and his wife, a teacher at your church or friends.

Make it personal ___ 🖉

Did your parents provide you with a good example in parts or all of their marriage? If so, how?

Do you know people with good marriages? Who are they? What do you like about their relationships?

Look for the positive in your mate.

Have you become a negative person, frequently noticing your spouse's faults? If so, you aren't alone. Most of us tend to focus on the negative. Train yourself, instead, to look for the positive—those things about your spouse that are true, noble, right, pure, lovely, admirable, excellent, or praiseworthy. Although your marriage may not yet resemble God's ideal picture, you will discover that looking for the positive moves you in the right direction.

 Finally, brothers, whatever is true, whatever is noble, whatever is right, whatever is pure, whatever is lovely, whatever is admirable—if anything is excellent or praiseworthy—think about such things. (Philippians 4:8)

Make it personal ____ 🖉

Think about your spouse in the light of Philippians 4:8. Write ways he or she is true, noble, right, pure, lovely, admirable, excellent, or praiseworthy.

There is Hope for Your Marriage

If you are desperately unhappy in your marriage, please do not despair. I have seen even the most disastrous marriages beautifully transformed. As you turn to God and apply his principles, you will see a change.

God can do miracles in spite of your situation. As Paul wrote, God *"is able to do immeasurably more than all we ask or imagine, according to his power that is at work within us"* *(Ephesians 3:20).* Let the following Scriptures encourage you:

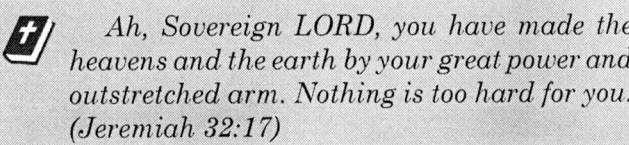

> *Ah, Sovereign LORD, you have made the heavens and the earth by your great power and outstretched arm. Nothing is too hard for you. (Jeremiah 32:17)*

> *With man this is impossible, but with God all things are possible. (Matthew 19:26)*

No matter how bad your relationship is, if even one of you puts God's principles into practice, there is an excellent chance your marriage will improve wondrously. If both of you decide to roll up your sleeves and go to work, you can count on miracles.

Make it personal ___ 🖉

Talk to God: *"Lord, sometimes the obstacles we face seem overwhelming. But I know you have the power to overcome every one of them. Please help me walk in the knowledge of your hope and power, in Jesus' name.*
Check this box after you pray: ☐

Putting It All Together — Chapter 1

Key point: Pray that God will help you deeply understand what it means to be "one flesh."

Memory verse: *"'The two will become one flesh.' So they are no longer two, but one." (Mark 10:8)*

Action plan: Choose one or two lessons from this chapter to work on this week:

1.

2.

Chapter 2
Focus on Changes
You Should Make

*Why do you look at the speck of sawdust in your brother's
eye and pay no attention to the plank in
your own eye? (Matthew 7:3)*

Martha's voice grew louder as she sat across from me in
my counseling office. "All he wants is a maid. He doesn't
listen to what I say, and he certainly doesn't love me." Her
husband Tom, seated next to her, saw things differently. "I'm
a good listener," he said, "and I love her very much. The whole
problem is that she's such a negative person."

Neither one saw how he or she contributed to their problems, yet each played a part. It didn't take long before it became obvious that Martha herself was a poor listener. She
talked incessantly and showed little interest in what Tom
said. He, on the other hand, did not understand that his long
hours away from home and lack of attention contributed to
her feeling unloved.

Tom and Martha are typical. When I first see a couple for
counseling, the husband usually says something like, "Doug,
if you can fix my wife, we'll have a good marriage." And, of
course, the wife says, "Doug, if you can fix my husband we'll
have a good marriage."

Have you ever elbowed your spouse in church when the
minister said exactly what you thought he or she needed to
hear? Chances are that you, like most of us, think your marriage would improve if your spouse would change.

Examples of blaming the other person abound. Here are
some instances from my counseling office:

- Ted often complained about his wife's housekeeping, yet was blind to how his criticisms affected her.

- Mary frequently chewed out her husband for not going to church. She did not hear how hypocritical she sounded as she yelled at him to be a better Christian.

- Lance often screamed awful things at his wife, yet blamed her for his anger. He was mad, he said, because she was not sweet and romantic.

  He justified his anger, saying that if she would act more lovingly, he would be the best husband in the world. He had no idea that his anger was short-circuiting her desire to express love.

- Rick was physically abusive. He saw nothing wrong with his logic when he said, "I wouldn't hit her if she didn't make me do it by burning the toast."

Women who are violent—and there are more of them than you might think—have similar excuses. Jennifer said, "Yes, I hit him. But I didn't hit hard." She went on to justify her violence, saying she was tired of being ignored.

It is easy and natural to focus on others' faults. Seeing our own problems is more difficult and less comfortable. But God tells us to look first at changes *we* should make. Jesus emphasized this when he said:

 Why do you look at the speck of sawdust in your brother's eye and pay no attention to the plank in your own eye? How can you say to your brother, "Let me take the speck out of your eye," when all the time there is a plank in your own eye? You hypocrite, first take the plank out of your own eye, and then you will see clearly to remove the speck from your brother's eye. (Matthew 7:3-5)

Make it personal ___ ✐

Do you sometimes focus on changes your mate should make more than those you should make? ☐ Yes ☐ No

What might make it difficult for you to focus on changes *you* should make?

How will you overcome this tendency?

_____

"But my spouse is so irritating."

No matter who your spouse is, he or she has faults. Maybe he puts off mowing the lawn. Maybe she runs the car gas tank down to empty. Perhaps things happen that are much worse. However, even if your mate's actions are irritating, God wants you to focus on improving yourself first.

This makes a lot of sense if you think about it. Changing yourself is difficult. Getting your spouse to change is even harder.

Check the following statements that apply to you. Feel free to substitute "he," "his," "she," and "her" where appropriate.

☐ "I wish he were a better listener."

☐ "I'm embarrassed by her manners."

☐ "I don't like the way he dresses."

☐ "I get irritated at the way she drives."

☐ "I'm upset at all the TV he watches."

☐ "I wish she'd put the toilet paper roll on right."

☐ "I wish he talked more."

☐ "I wish she talked less."

☐ "I wish she were more romantic."

☐ "He says that just to annoy me."

☐ "Why won't she stop complaining?"

☐ "I can't stand the way he interrupts me."

☐ "She says the dumbest things!"

☐ "My spouse makes me mad."

Make it personal ___ ✎

Read Ephesians 4:29-32 and Colossians 3:12-13. How do these verses tell us to respond if we are irritated?

Now look at the boxes you checked in the previous section. Choose one of them and write how you will apply Ephesians 4:29-32 and Colossians 3:12-13 instead of giving in to anger or resentment.

Talk to God: *"Lord, please forgive my bitterness and help me learn how to live with an imperfect spouse with grace and love, in Jesus' name."*
Check this box after you pray: ☐

Identify Your Excuses

The following are excuses we sometimes give for not taking the plank out of our own eye, and why they are just that—excuses. As you read, ask yourself if you have had these thoughts, and then check each one that applies to you. (Remember that each excuse applies equally to husband and wife.)

☐ **"I'll look at myself when he looks at himself."**
You may think that since you and your mate are one flesh, you should change together. If so, you are partially right. Ideally, you and your spouse will strive to improve together. It is wonderful when a couple shares a vision of a beautiful marriage and works together to bring it to pass.

However, don't simply say, "It takes two to tango." Whether or not your spouse joins you in trying to improve your marriage, God expects *you* to become the best husband or wife you can be. Be encouraged by the fact that when one partner works to improve, the other often is inspired to change.

☐ **"It's all his fault."**

It's unlikely that it's all your spouse's fault! It is extremely rare that one person is completely right and the other is all wrong. Adam blamed his wife when God confronted his sin (Genesis 3:11-12), but God did not accept his excuse (Genesis 3:17-19). Nor will God accept your excuses.

Honestly confront and seek to eliminate your own faults, even if you think you are only one percent wrong and your spouse is ninety-nine percent wrong.

☐ **"He makes me angry."**

One of the most common variations of "It's all his fault" is, "He makes me so angry. I would be able to hold my temper if he weren't so awful."

Yet the Bible says, *"Do not repay anyone evil for evil" (Romans 12:17).* It continues, *"Do not be overcome by evil, but overcome evil with good" (Romans 12:21).* Regardless of what your spouse does, you are responsible for the way you respond.

You will have a miserable life if you do not accept your bad temper as a personal problem. Why? Because your mate is imperfect, and you always will be able to find an excuse to be angry.

Decide to do something about your anger. Confess that you have a problem, ask forgiveness, and learn how to overcome it.

☐ **"I need to confront her sin."**

Sometimes you may need to bring up your spouse's sin, but this should be rare. When you think you should confront your mate, look again at Matthew 7:3-5 and you will see three points:

- *You must first take the plank out of your own eye.* Deal with your own sins.

- *Until you take the plank out of your own eye, you cannot see clearly.* How can you trust your insights, observations, and opinions when your sight is blocked?

- *Once you confront your own sins, you can remove the speck from your mate's eye.* You will be able to do so accurately—and lovingly.

An eye is vulnerable, tender, and easily damaged. If you try to remove the speck from your spouse's eye without first taking the plank out of your own eye, you cannot see clearly and will hurt your spouse.

Paul made a similar point when he wrote, *"Brothers, if someone is caught in a sin, you who are spiritual should restore him gently" (Galatians 6:1).* Notice that only those who are spiritual should try to restore others. Also notice that the restoration is to be done gently.

☐ **"He'll take advantage of me."**

You may fear that if you focus on changes you should make, your spouse will take advantage of you. Although that is possible, it is not likely. The most common result is just the opposite. The changes you make usually inspire your spouse also to change. When Skeeter treats me sweetly, it makes me want to be a better husband. Likewise, she says that seeing me put effort into our marriage inspires her to be a better wife.

However, it is possible, although unlikely, that your spouse will take advantage of your kindness and ask you to do more and more. If this happens, gently point it out. Explain that you want to be the best spouse possible, but you cannot do everything. Identify those things that are most important to your mate and work on addressing them, but do not try to do everything he or she desires.

Make it personal ____ 🖉

Do you use these or any other excuses to avoid focusing on yourself? ☐ Yes ☐ No

If you checked "yes," what are your excuses?

If you did not hide behind these excuses, what would you do differently?

Evaluate Yourself by the Bible

It is difficult to see yourself clearly. As the Bible says, *"All a man's ways seem innocent to him, but motives are weighed by the LORD" (Proverbs 16:2).*

The heart of marriage is love. One way to identify changes you need to make is to read these verses from 1 Corinthians 13, and then take the following quiz.

Love is patient, love is kind. It does not envy, it does not boast, it is not proud. It is not rude, it is not self-seeking, it is not easily angered, it keeps no record of wrongs. Love does not delight in evil but rejoices with the truth. It always protects, always trusts, always hopes, always perseveres. Love never fails. (1 Corinthians 13:4-8)

How well do you practice 1 Corinthians 13? Rate yourself from 0 to 10 on each part of God's definition of love.

- "0" means, "I need a lot of improvement."
- "10" means, "I do this very well."

	My score (0-10)
I am patient.	___
I am kind.	___
I do not envy.	___
I do not boast.	___
I am not proud.	___
I am not rude.	___
I am not self-seeking.	___
I am not easily angered.	___
I keep no record of wrongs.	___
I do not delight in evil.	___
I rejoice with the truth.	___
I always protect.	___
I always trust.	___
I always hope.	___
I always persevere.	___
My love never fails.	___

Make it personal ___ 🖋

What changes would you like to make in light of 1 Corinthians 13:4-8?

Talk to God: *"God, I have not loved as you have instructed. Please forgive me and give me the grace to make the changes I need to make. I ask this in Jesus' name."*
Check this box after you pray: ☐

Take Special Care in Tense Times

It's hard to examine your own attitude in the middle of an argument or when discussing high-tension topics. It is *really* difficult when you are criticized or think you are mistreated or misunderstood. Most of us fight back, attacking the other person. Yet even at these tense times, God says to first take the plank out of your own eye.

Ask the Lord to help you *respond* with wisdom and love, not *react* in the flesh. Remember the verses, *"Bless those who persecute you; bless and do not curse"(Romans 12:14)* and, *"Do not be overcome by evil, but overcome evil with good"(Romans 12:21).*

The following guidelines will help you keep the right focus when problems come up.

Thank God for the opportunity to learn and grow.

James showed us how to react to hard times in these remarkable verses:

 Consider it pure joy, my brothers, whenever you face trials of many kinds, because you know that the testing of your faith develops perseverance. Perseverance must finish its work so that you may be mature and complete, not lacking anything. (James 1:2-4)

James had emotions like everyone else. He knew that we do not automatically *feel* joyful in trials, so he told us to *consider* it pure joy when we go through hard times. His goal was to teach us a way to bring good from suffering. Paul gave us similar instructions in Romans 5:3-4 and 2 Corinthians 12:10.

This principle has helped me many times. I often remind myself to thank God when problems come up, seeing them as opportunities to learn how to be a better husband.

If you have not already begun to practice this principle, start today. If your mate greets you with harsh words after work, praise God silently in your mind, thinking, "Thank you, God, for this opportunity to grow in patience and wisdom."

Do not say to your mate, "Look at yourself."

If your spouse criticizes you, it may be tempting to say, "You're supposed to look at yourself." Even if your mate is out of line, if you say this you are violating the principle of focusing on yourself. If he or she criticizes you, be humble and listen. Ask God to help you learn from the complaint.

Rarely quote this book to your spouse.

It may be tempting to quote things you read to your mate, pointing out his or her shortcomings. Avoid that temptation, since it usually leads to quarrels. Remember to focus on yourself.

Ask yourself these questions:
If you find yourself in an argument with your spouse, or if you find yourself feeling upset about something he or she did, ask yourself:

- **Did I contribute to the problem?**
  It is hard to see our own faults clearly. I have often been sure Skeeter was the only one with the problem, only to look back days, weeks, or even years later to realize how wrong and immature I had been.
  Our own role in a problem is not always immediately obvious. For example, one time Skeeter told me her opinion about a decision facing us. I thought her points were good, but didn't say so. A few days later, she brought up the conversation and said, "Doug, you never listen to me."
  At first, I was confused because I had listened to her and actually had changed my mind as a result. But as we talked, I realized two ways I had contributed to her distress. In our original discussion, I had silently listened but had not said anything to show I was paying attention or that I had changed my position. On top of that, I had not talked with her much for several days before our conversation, and she felt neglected.
  You too may have trouble seeing your part in a problem. Ask God to help you. Also ask your spouse to tell you how he or she sees your role in the situation. As you become aware of how your thoughts, emotions, actions, and words affect your mate, you will discover that you contribute to problems more than you realize.

- **How can I help in this conversation?**
  Seek to serve your spouse in the midst of the discussion. For example, when Skeeter said, "Doug, you never listen to me," I made it my goal to listen in-

tently. The next morning, I asked how she felt about our relationship. She responded, "Great! You listened to me last night."

- **How does God want me to speak?**

    God wants us to speak with love and courtesy, whatever the circumstances. Our words should be things of beauty, *"like apples of gold in settings of silver" (Proverbs 25:11)*. Words spoken in haste or anger are hard to take back.

Make it personal ____ ✐

Briefly summarize an argument you had with your mate when you were sure you were right.

Review the guidelines in this section and then write how you contributed to the problem.

Choose one of the above guidelines and make a plan to practice it this week.

- Which guideline will you put into practice?

- Describe the type of situation in which you will apply this guideline.

Stay Balanced

God wants you to focus on changes you should make. But if you are not careful, you can misapply this principle and get into trouble. The following suggestions will help you avoid common pitfalls.

Do not blame yourself for everything.

Don't take the principle of focusing on yourself too far and blame yourself for everything that goes wrong. Your spouse is a human being and probably contributed to the problems. It is okay to be aware that he or she has faults. Just don't dwell on them or excuse your sins because of them.

If your mate sins, and then says it is your fault, evaluate how you may have contributed to the problem, but do not accept all the blame. Even if you contributed, your spouse is responsible before God for his or her actions.

Make it personal ___ ✐

Do you blame yourself for your spouse's anger or other faults?
☐ Yes ☐ No

If so, what is a more accurate view?

Talk about your ideas and desires from time to time.

Some think that the principles I have been writing about mean we should never express personal desires or opinions. They think that by always keeping quiet they are demonstrating godly love.

That is not what God had in mind when he created Adam and Eve to rule together (Genesis 1:28). The ideas and opinions of both marriage partners are important. When Skeeter and I share our thoughts, we make a better team.

When you discuss your ideas and desires, do so politely and respectfully. Avoid nagging.

Discuss problems from time to time.

Along similar lines, some people never discuss tough subjects because they don't want to sound critical. This is a mistake. The New Testament records many times when difficult subjects were discussed. Study, for example, Acts 15:1-12.

Although these verses are not about marriage, they show that it is okay to talk about real issues. Such conversations can bring you closer together. Here are some guidelines:

- **Do not complain too much.**
  If you complain too often, you risk becoming a nag. *"A quarrelsome wife is like a constant dripping on a rainy day" (Proverbs 27:15).*

- **Bring up your complaints wisely.**
  The way you introduce a topic makes a big difference in how well your spouse responds. Speak as a friend, not as an enemy.

- **Speak courteously.**
  Remember Galatians 6:1. Speak gently in even the most difficult discussions.

- **Seek to understand your spouse's point of view.**
  Although you are bringing up a concern of your own, be a good listener. Try to see through your mate's eyes.

Make it personal ___ 🖉

Fred forgot the last two dinner dates he made with his wife Paula. It's Friday night and he's outside working on the car. He seems to have forgotten once again. Paula doesn't want to be a nag. What should she do?

Take strong actions if necessary.
How do you think a Christian should respond to abusive behavior? Does God want you to have a victim's mentality, passively accepting every kind of mistreatment? No. The Bible instructs us to love (1 John 3:11) and seek wisdom (Proverbs 1:20-22, 2:1-6). At times, the most loving and wise action is to take a strong defensive stand.

Do not allow physical abuse. If it occurs, call your pastor, get a temporary restraining order, or file criminal charges if necessary. Read in Acts 25:10-11 about how Paul claimed the protection of the Roman law when he was persecuted.

If you take strong protective actions, focus on your attitude and *how* you take these steps. Ask God to help you act with integrity and love.

Make it personal ___ ✏

Do you need to take strong actions because of abusive behavior?
☐ Yes ☐ No

What actions will you take? How? When?

Do your best, and then leave the results to God. Do not take sole responsibility for your spouse's happiness. Although God expects you to be the best husband or wife you can be, you are not responsible for the results. You cannot control your spouse. Once you do your part, put him or her in God's hands.

Make it personal ___ ✐

Do you take responsibility for results that you should leave in God's hands? ☐ Yes ☐ No

If you answered "yes," describe one situation in which this was true. What will you do differently next time?

Always Keep Learning

Those who succeed on the job attend seminars, take classes, and read manuals to gain new knowledge and skills. They constantly evaluate their actions, looking for better ways to do things.

You and I need to approach marriage the same way, always seeking to learn how to become a better spouse. Study the Word of God, pay attention to your emotions, examine your motives, observe your actions, and listen to your words. Always be ready to learn.

Pray for insight.

Ask God to help you see how to become a better spouse. If you and your mate have a disagreement, ask the Lord to help you see your part.

Ask, "How did I do?"

After discussing a difficult subject, sometimes ask your spouse, "How did I do in this conversation?" Or at the end of the day, ask, "How did I do today?"

Listen to the answer without becoming defensive. Do not start a fight by discounting what your mate says or reacting with anger or hurt feelings. Instead, seek to truly understand your spouse.

However, if your mate bitterly levels attack after attack, ask him or her to slow down and give a two or three sentence summary. Then thank your spouse for the feedback and end the conversation on as positive a note as possible.

Ask a friend for feedback.

It can be difficult to see how you contribute to a problem or what you could do differently. If you still are confused after praying and talking with your mate, consider asking a Christian friend for suggestions.

If you decide to talk with someone, choose a mature, trustworthy person of the same sex, one who is not a gossip. Make it clear that you want to talk about what *you* should do, not criticize your mate. Choose a friend who will confront you instead of simply taking your side.

Do not be crushed by self-criticism.

When you examine yourself, you are sure to find faults. Everyone, including you (and me!), is imperfect. Don't sink into depression because of this. Instead, let the knowledge of your shortcomings inspire you to change. To borrow from Paul's words, choose godly sorrow, not worldly sorrow.

 Godly sorrow brings repentance that leads to salvation and leaves no regret, but worldly sorrow brings death. (2 Corinthians 7:10)

As you confront your shortcomings, remember God's love, mercy and grace.

Watch out for self-pity.

If you put your whole heart into doing the right thing, only to have things blow up in your face, you might start feeling sorry for yourself. That's understandable, yet don't give in to bitterness or self-pity. Say a prayer, forgive your mate, and evaluate the situation to learn what to do differently next time.

Make it personal ___ ✏

How frequently do you evaluate yourself as a husband or wife?

How frequently should you evaluate yourself? Why?

Putting It All Together — Chapter 2

Key point: Become the best husband or wife possible regardless of what your spouse says or does.

Memory verse: *"Why do you look at the speck of sawdust in your brother's eye and pay no attention to the plank in your own eye?" (Matthew 7:3)*

Action plan: Choose one or two lessons from this chapter to work on this week:

1.

2.

Chapter 3
Throw Yourself into Your Marriage

Whatever you do, work at it with all your heart, as working for the Lord, not for men. (Colossians 3:23)

Imagine telling a football coach, "I want to be the quarterback, but don't expect me to go to training camp, read playbooks, lift weights, or practice. I'll just do what comes naturally." You wouldn't make the team.

It takes hard work to succeed at almost anything. Someone who desires to earn ten million dollars works long hours and makes many sacrifices. Someone who wants to win a marathon trains intensely. And someone who wishes to excel in school burns the midnight oil.

The same is true of smaller projects. Some people spend many hours every week keeping a tidy house, maintaining an immaculate lawn, or keeping up-to-date on the statistics of their favorite sports team.

Yet these same people often put little effort into building their marriage. They think that being married is simple, that everything should come naturally. Or they look at getting married like catching a fish. Once you catch the fish, there's no need to go to any more effort, is there? Why keep trying to entice it with fancy lures when you already have it in your hands?

You may have thought that being married would come naturally, so after the wedding you changed your priorities. Now you wonder why your marriage is in trouble. One reason may be that you have not put enough time and attention into creating a great marriage.

Make it personal ___ ✐

What sort of effort do you put into being a great husband or wife? Do you throw yourself into it, or are you like the lazy football player?

Put Your Spouse Before All Others

Most of Sylvia's friends thought she was a wonderful person. Whenever she had free time, she was on the phone counseling someone in need. But her husband Marcus felt abandoned. Although they were often home together, they rarely talked or did things as a couple.

Louise, too, felt abandoned. Her husband Dan spent most of his time playing sports with his buddies. He seemed to look at marriage as a part-time activity.

It's no wonder both of these marriages were floundering. The Bible tells us to be "united" or to "cleave" to our spouse (Genesis 2:24). To cleave means to tightly hold on to each other. It requires much thought, creativity, effort, and prayer. It requires action. It is a commitment not just to stay together, but also to work at developing and maintaining an intimate relationship.

The good news is that this work is not gritting-your-teeth-and-doing-something-unpleasant work. It is talking, going on walks, and playing. It is complimenting and showing respect. It is listening. It is going on dates. It is (usually) fun.

Does this mean you must be together all the time? No, it's okay to read, help others, spend time with friends, watch television or enjoy hobbies on your own—but only if you have first thrown yourself into marriage-building activities. Your investment of time and effort will pay off.

Make it personal _____ 🖉

Evaluate your priorities. What are the most important things in your life?

Do you see inconsistencies between what you say is important and how you spend your time? If so, what are they?

What changes will you make?

_____

Do Not Take Your Mate for Granted

The message of this chapter does not only apply to those with marriage problems. It also speaks to those who enjoy rewarding relationships. It certainly holds true for Skeeter and me. When things go along pretty well, I find it easy to stop working on our marriage. I have to discipline myself not to slip into cruise control.

I remember a time when I fell into a destructive pattern. Over a period of several months, I would withdraw emotionally, spending little time talking about things that mattered. Tension would build in Skeeter until she exploded. Then we would talk intensely for a few days until the pressure lifted. Once things seemed okay, I would say to myself, "I'm glad that's taken care of," and proceed to repeat the pattern. We went through this cycle several times before I realized that marriage requires ongoing communication.

Many couples fall into a similar trap. After working hard and seeing their marriage improve, they become complacent and drift back into the same patterns that got them into trouble in the first place.

Join me in fighting marriage laziness. Pray for God's help. Talk together daily about what matters in your lives. Practice listening. Go on dates. Do whatever it takes. Refuse to turn on the cruise control.

Make it personal ___ 🖋

Are you lazy when things are okay? ☐ Yes ☐ No

What will you do to avoid this?

Watch What You Sacrifice

People often talk about sacrificing for their marriage. What they often mean by this is that they work long hours to make lots of money, maybe holding down two jobs or putting in huge amounts of overtime.

Other people sacrifice time with their mate to minister to others' needs. Some pastors, for instance, rarely eat at home because they are busy helping members of their flock.

Philip said he was sacrificing for his family. He worked many hours of overtime every week so his wife and children could have a better home. But it seemed to them as if he were saying, "You're the most important people in the world to me. That's why I'm never home."

They wanted *him*, not a nicer home. His wife became lonely and bitter. He felt unappreciated, and they ended up divorcing. He sacrificed the wrong thing—time with his family.

Philip is not unique. Countless business owners, attorneys, waiters, carpenters, teachers, volunteers, politicians, doctors, pastors, farmers, and others make the same mistake. They sacrifice time with their mate for the sake of their job.

Melinda made a different type of sacrifice, one that also hurt her marriage. She said she was too busy to talk with her husband Edward or to make love on school nights. Her reason? Their children were having trouble in school, so she felt compelled to ignore him and spend hours every night helping them with homework. Edward expressed his desire to spend time with her and offered to help with the kids' schoolwork. Unfortunately, Melinda insisted it was her duty to sacrifice everything and spend all her time with the kids. Edward felt abandoned.

We need to make the right kind of sacrifices. We should be willing to give up earning a giant salary, being the best on the job, buying a new car, or living in a big house. We may need to stop helping others so much to give ourselves more time with our spouse.

Are there ever times when it is okay to sacrifice time together? Sure. There are exceptions. But before making them, be certain you both agree, it is for a relatively short time. and you spend at least some high-quality time together every day.

Make it personal ___ 🖉

Do you tend to make the wrong sacrifices? ☐ Yes ☐ No

If you checked "yes," talk with your mate. Make a plan to rear-range your schedules.

Overcome Excuses

There are countless reasons we give for not throwing our-selves into our marriage. Here are three I often hear when counseling couples.

"My spouse isn't trying, so why should I?"

People often say that their spouse is not working to im-prove their relationship. Sometimes this is true, but I have known many occasions in which the complaining spouse was blind to the other person's efforts. If you are certain you are the only one trying, you likely overlook evidence that may prove you wrong.

However, even if your spouse really has stopped trying, God expects you to roll up your sleeves and go to work at be-coming the best husband or wife possible. As Paul wrote, *"Serve wholeheartedly, as if you were serving the Lord, not men" (Ephesians 6:7).*

Jennifer found herself needing to put this principle into practice several years ago. Her husband Mike was continuously angry with her, but refused to come to counseling. She came by herself, determined to learn what she could do in spite of his unwillingness. As we talked, she learned several things she could work on and threw herself into doing them. When Mike saw her change, he too began to work at improving their marriage.

Make it personal ___ ✎

Will you work on your marriage wholeheartedly, as unto the Lord, regardless of how your spouse acts? ☐ Yes ☐ No

What changes do you need to make in your attitude or behavior?

"I don't feel close to him (or her)."

I can feel close to Skeeter in the morning, then more distant later in the day. If I were to base the way I act on how I feel, she would never know what to expect from me.

Our emotions are fickle. When we base our decisions on them, we often say and do things that harm our marriage.

If you don't feel close to your mate, don't wait for your feelings to change. Instead, throw yourself into your marriage. You will experience the joy that comes from obeying God, plus there's an excellent chance you will end up feeling closer to your husband or wife.

Make it personal ___ 🖉

Which has greater rule over you, God's Word or your emotions?

If your emotions cause you to pull back from throwing yourself into your marriage, write a prayer asking God to help you obey him, not your emotions.

"Our children are in trouble and need our help."
Jonas and Beth were deeply concerned for their daughter Lucy and her two children. Lucy was living a drug and alcohol-dominated life. She was a single mom, raising her children in a chaotic and squalid environment. She moved frequently and was sometimes homeless.

Now and then she and the kids dropped into Jonas and Beth's small home and lived with them. Other times, Lucy left the kids there and traveled.

It was crowded and tense when everyone lived in the small house, yet Jonas and Beth also found themselves tense when everyone was gone. They constantly feared the worst.

They became so consumed with worry about Lucy and their grandchildren that they neglected their marriage. They rarely talked about anything else, never went out, and seldom had fun together. Beth felt alone, as if she were not married. She sank into a deep depression and eventually sought counseling.

It is understandable that Jonas and Beth became enmeshed in this difficult situation. They loved their daughter and grandchildren and desired the best for them. Yet they needed to learn that in times of crisis we must make time to nurture our marriage. This is true regardless of the nature of the crisis, whether it is an emergency at work, the illness of a child, a family tragedy, or an ailing parent.

If you neglect your marriage during a time of crisis, the extra pressure of the emergency can destroy your marriage. This, of course, will make the crisis even worse. On the other hand, if you make an effort to strengthen your marriage during hard times, you will be able to deal with the extra pressures as a team.

When your world seems to be collapsing, spend time together. Pray. Talk about something other than the problems. Take walks. Tell jokes. Go on dates.

Make it personal ____ 🖋

Have you allowed a crisis to take too much time or energy away from your marriage? ☐ Yes ☐ No

If this has been true, what will you do differently?

Identify Steps *You* will Take

What changes should you personally make in your lifestyle to improve your marriage? Read the following checklist to identify activities that rob your marriage of energy and time. As you read, check the changes you plan to make.

Notice that the activities on this checklist are things *you* can do on your own. As I wrote earlier, work wholeheartedly on building your marriage relationship even if your spouse doesn't seem interested in it, *"as if you were serving the Lord, not men" (Ephesians 6:7).*

To spend more time together, I will:

☐   Stop bringing so much work home.

☐   Say "no" to overtime more often.

☐   Quit my second job and live more simply.

- ☐ Change my work schedule to be home when my spouse is.
- ☐ Spend less time on the computer.
- ☐ Allow the house to be a little less tidy.
- ☐ Cut back on my activities away from home.
- ☐ Watch less television.
- ☐ Study a little less, settling for B's instead of A's.
- ☐ Go to the gym less often.
- ☐ Stop going to church *every* night.
- ☐ Spend less time with friends or talking on the phone.
- ☐ Get involved in some of my spouse's activities.
- ☐ Spend less time helping the kids with their homework, activities, or sports.
- ☐ Help with the kids and housework, so my mate has more free time to spend with me.
- ☐ Minister to others less and my spouse more.
- ☐ Additional plan: _____
- ☐ Additional plan: _____
- ☐ Additional plan: _____

_____

Make it personal ___ ✐

What are some of *your* activities that interfere with your marriage?

Write plans to make changes in two of the problem areas you identified.

Plan 1:

Plan 2:

Do at least one marriage-building activity every day.

Make it your goal to reach out to your spouse in at least one way every day.

Ask God to help you identify what's special to your mate. Also ask your spouse what's important to him or her. It's possible to put a lot of energy into things that don't matter.

Here are a few ways you could reach out:

- Write a love note.

- Initiate a conversation.

- Phone from work to say, "I love you."

- Ask if you can pray together.
- Invite your spouse to go on a date.
- Offer to help with a household project.

Once you decide to engage in at least one marriage-building activity a day, how will you remember to follow through? One way could be to keep a calendar on which you record ways you reach out. Another could be to develop a habit of praying on the way home after work, asking the Lord to help you remember to reach out that night.

Make it personal ___ ✐

How will you be sure to reach out to your spouse daily?

Make Plans with Your Spouse

Now that you have made marriage-building plans you personally are going to carry out, talk with your spouse to see if he or she would like to make some plans as a team.

Before getting together, go over the following checklist and make a list of things you would like to do with your husband or wife.

I would like us to:

☐ Set aside a specific time to talk daily.

☐ Cook dinner together.

☐ Turn off the television and talk during dinner.

☐ Study the Bible together.

☐ Work together on a ministry.

☐ Do housework together.

☐ Go on walks.

☐ Join an organization, club, or sports team together.

☐ Go on dates.

☐ Additional idea: _____

☐ Additional idea: _____

☐ Additional idea: _____

Ask your spouse to complete the same checklist, and then set up a time to talk. When you meet, ask what he or she would like to do together before sharing your ideas. Keep talking until you identify something you both would like to do.

Make a plan.

If you are like many people, you and your mate may say you'd like to spend more time together, but you put off doing anything because you think you are too busy. You might say, "Things will calm down next month. Then we'll have more time." If you aren't careful, months or years may go by with nothing changing.

Don't simply say, "We ought to spend more time together." Good intentions are not enough. Make specific plans.

Make it personal ___ ✐

Talk with your spouse and write what you plan to do together this week.

Now write what might spoil your plan—and how you will overcome that obstacle.

_____

Plan for both to get enough sleep.

My sleep patterns have hindered my ability to be a good husband. I work hard during the day and like to stay up late at night, both to write and to read. The result? Sometimes I am so tired that I have little energy for my marriage.

I am not alone in this. When Skeeter and I led a marriage group in our church, many cited exhaustion as the major reason for neglecting their marriage. They were so tired that they counted it a success if they managed to be polite to each other.

God's Word warns in many places against laziness. Yet it also tells us to get enough sleep.

 In vain you rise early and stay up late, toiling for food to eat—for he grants sleep to those he loves. (Psalm 127:2)

Go to bed early enough to get the sleep you need. Turn off the TV. Put the book down. Stop doing paperwork.

Make it personal ___ ✎

Do you sleep enough? ☐ Yes ☐ No

If not, how will you change?

Does your spouse sleep enough? ☐ Yes ☐ No

If not, ask if there is any way you could help him or her get more sleep.

Persevere

When you commit to building a great marriage, you will run into obstacles. Your old nature will resist your efforts (Romans 7:14-18). Your spouse may not respond the way you'd like. Your schedule may be packed solid. Changing is hard work. Do not give up. Instead, persevere.

> *You need to persevere so that when you have done the will of God, you will receive what he has promised. (Hebrews 10:36)*

> *Let us run with perseverance the race marked out for us. (Hebrews 12:1)*

Make it personal ___ ✐

Look up the following verses on perseverance: Romans 5:3-4; Hebrews 10:36, 11:27, and 12:1-3; James 1:12 and 5:10-11, and Revelation 2:19.

Write out one of these verses that speaks to you.

Putting It All Together — Chapter 3

Key point: Throw yourself into building your marriage every day.

Memory verse: *"Whatever you do, work at it with all your heart, as working for the Lord, not for men." (Colossians 3:23)*

Action plan: Choose one or two lessons from this chapter to work on this week:

1.

2.

Chapter 4
Commit to Your Marriage

Therefore what God has joined together, let man not separate. (Matthew 19:6)

Complete commitment to your marriage provides a foundation of dependability and trust. It takes you through tough times and steers you toward godly solutions. A lack of commitment erodes your strength, determination, and resourcefulness. It can lead to tragedy.

What do I mean by commitment? It is a solid promise to stay in your marriage and make it the best one possible, no matter what the obstacles. It is a determination not to divorce unless there are biblical grounds.

You may think, "Oh, oh. This chapter is going to be rough" because you have struggled with thoughts of divorce, or perhaps you have divorced in the past. Although it may be hard, keep reading. You will find yourself strengthened and encouraged to live a holy and righteous life.

Even if divorce seems unimaginable to you, let me urge you to read this chapter to arm yourself against possible future trials. Most people who divorce never imagined they would, but found their attitudes changing as they went through rough times. It is possible your marriage will go through a deep crisis and, to your shock, you may find yourself thinking about divorce. By studying this chapter, you will prepare yourself against such temptations.

Marriage can be compared to a marathon race. If you don't commit yourself to running the distance no matter what the cost, your chances of dropping out along the way increase. But if you are determined, you will find unforeseen strength to overcome every obstacle.

Embrace God's attitude about divorce.

The Bible says that when two are joined together in marriage, they are no longer two, but one, and that God hates divorce. You and your spouse are "one" no matter how poorly your marriage is functioning. Divorce, in God's eyes, is not an option except in specific situations—and even then, forgiveness and rebuilding are usually best.

Study these Scriptures to see how serious the Lord is about divorce:

 "I hate divorce," says the LORD God of Israel. (Malachi 2:16)

What God has joined together, let man not separate ... I tell you that anyone who divorces his wife, except for marital unfaithfulness, and marries another woman commits adultery. (Matthew 19:6, 9)

Anyone who divorces his wife and marries another woman commits adultery against her. And if she divorces her husband and marries another man, she commits adultery. (Mark 10:11-12)

If any brother has a wife who is not a believer and she is willing to live with him, he must not divorce her. And if a woman has a husband who is not a believer and he is willing to live with her, she must not divorce him. (1 Corinthians 7:12-13)

Do not let your commitment to your spouse be like a yo-yo, going up and down depending on your feelings. Deal with your problems without considering divorce. Determine to do things God's way, regardless of how you feel.

> *Trust in the LORD with all your heart and lean not on your own understanding. (Proverbs 3:5)*

Skeeter and I probably would not be married today if God allowed divorce. As we look back, each of us can remember times early in our marriage, even after we became Christians, when we were disgusted and frustrated with each other, times when we both wanted out. But neither of us sought divorce because we knew it was sinful. This knowledge held us together through difficult years and pushed us to improve our marriage. Now, as we enjoy a happy marriage, we are grateful for God's commands against divorce. We needed them. You need them too.

Don't rebel against God.

It is hard to overstate how much God hates divorce. Jesus said that to divorce for unscriptural reasons and then remarry is to commit adultery. Yet many people who profess Christianity play games with God by divorcing and then cruising along as if God did not mind. They often continue to attend church and engage in "spiritual" activities or ministries, thinking everything is fine. They look good on the outside. But read what God says about them:

> *You flood the Lord's altar with tears. You weep and wail because he no longer pays attention to your offerings or accepts them with pleasure from your hands. You ask, "Why?" It is because the LORD is acting as the witness between you and the wife of your youth, because you have broken faith with her, though she is your partner, the wife of your marriage covenant. (Malachi 2:13-14)*

In other words, when you divorce for unscriptural reasons, you drive a wedge between yourself and God, for you are rebelling against him.

Realize that divorce has consequences.

Unscriptural divorce always brings painful consequences. Not only do you distance yourself from God when you divorce, you also damage your spouse, wound your children, injure other family members, hurt friends, set the stage for future pain for yourself, and bring shame upon the name of Christ.

When you do things God's way, things work out best. On the other hand, when you disobey God, problems eventually come. If you divorce for unscriptural reasons, the odds are high that you will regret it before you die. You are certain to regret it when you stand before God.

Make it personal ___ 🖋

Have you looked at divorce as a possibility in spite of what the Bible says? ☐ Yes ☐ No

If so, in what ways do you need to change your attitude?

Unscriptural Excuses for Divorce

Although the Bible is clear about divorce, many of us have been sorely tempted by thoughts of it. Some have relatively minor reasons, such as "He always watches sports on television," or, "She gained forty pounds."

Others are devastated because they have been criticized day after day or have lost a home because of a spouse's drug habit. It's easy to understand why people in these situations might want to end their marriage.

Yet God's position against divorce is unmistakable. The following are some common, unscriptural justifications people give for divorce. Feel free to substitute "he" or "she" where appropriate.

As you read, ask yourself if you ever say or think any of these things. If you do, ask God for forgiveness and strength to look at things his way.

"I married the wrong person."

Maybe you did marry the "wrong" person. If so, you are not alone. Many of us married someone we should not have, married under poor circumstances, or married at the wrong time.

But even if you sinned when you married, you cannot fix it by divorcing, for you would be sinning again. Read the example of David and Bathsheba (2 Samuel 11-12). David had sexual relations with Bathsheba when she was married to someone else, arranged to have her husband killed, and then married her. This was a terrible way to start a marriage, and they suffered because of it.

Although David and Bathsheba's marriage started in sin, God did not tell them to divorce. In fact, read Matthew 1:6 and you will see that their son, Solomon, was one of Joseph's ancestors. (Joseph was the husband of Mary, mother of Jesus.) Although we may suffer terribly because of our choices (Galatians 6:7-8), God can bring unforeseen blessings out of our sins.

"I love someone else."
I remember one of the first times someone told me he was divorcing because he loved someone else. Jeremy had been active in his church for many years, but he planned to leave his wife and children because he thought he had fallen in love with a woman on the job.

He and his coworker had worked together on a project for several weeks. When it was completed, he took her to a celebration party at a friend's apartment, leaving his wife at home. They drank wine and danced. As Jeremy held her in his arms, he found himself "falling in love."

Since then, many other married men and women have told me of falling in love with someone else, someone they thought really listened and cared.

Mary was typical. Although she didn't like the way her husband treated her, she was not looking to get out of the marriage or have an affair. Yet she found herself becoming increasingly interested in a man who sat beside her week after week as she watched her son play in his youth sports league. (Her husband did not go to the games.)

This man seemed to really enjoy talking with her and was a great listener. At first she felt an emotional bond growing between them but was not interested in him sexually. Then one day his shoulder touched hers as they sat together. She did not pull away. One thing led to another, and she found herself "falling in love," having an affair and desiring a divorce.

You, too, may have met someone at work, the grocery store, or even church who seems more attentive and respectful than your spouse. The Bible gives clear instructions about how to deal with such situations:

- **Do not fantasize about sinning.**

    Do not think about past sins or plan how to sin in the future (Romans 13:14). Remember, Jesus said that to divorce and then marry someone else is to commit adultery (Matthew 19:9 and Mark 10:11-12). Resist the temptation, and concentrate your thoughts on what is right and pure (Philippians 4:8).

This also applies to daydreaming about people you dated before marrying. Don't fantasize about others or dwell on memories of past relationships. Instead, seek God's help to truly love your mate. In future years, you will be glad you chose righteousness.

- **Avoid tempting situations.**

Jeremy should have stayed home or taken his wife to the celebration party.

> *The highway of the upright avoids evil; he who guards his way guards his life. (Proverbs 16:17)*

- **Do not flirt.**

Avoid inappropriate comments, "innocently" touching others, or saying anything that could be interpreted as meaning you are available.

- **Be guided by true love, not emotional "love."**

Pray to understand true love that comes from God, not "love" that comes from your flesh. If you really love someone, you do not do anything that might cause him or her to sin. If Jeremy really loved his co-worker, he would not have attended the party—for her sake as well as his own.

- **Run when tempted.**

When opportunities for sin present themselves, run away. Paul told Timothy to *"flee the evil desires of youth" (2 Timothy 2:22).*

Study Genesis 39:6-23, verses that describe Joseph's flight from temptation. If you are involved in a potentially sinful relationship with someone else, be like Joseph: Flee! Make a complete break.

Do not play dangerous games with God by getting together for "innocent" reasons or talking on the phone as a "friend." Do the right thing, both for your-self and for the other person, by completely cutting off the relationship. Do not lay the foundation for trag-edy.

- **Throw all your energy into your marriage.**

   I am delighted you are reading this book, for in its pages you will discover many insights and practical suggestions to help you create a blessed marriage. Don't look for ways to get out of your marriage. In-stead, look for ways to improve it.

"I don't love my mate," or, "I've fallen out of love."

The Bible tells husbands to love their wives (Ephesians 5:25) and wives to love their husbands (Titus 2:4). Biblical love is seen primarily in our choices, attitudes, and actions, not in our emotions. True love is based on our promises to God and to each other, not on how we feel at the moment. People who fall in and out of "love" allow themselves to be controlled by their emotions and not by the Spirit of God.

Many marriages have been transformed when people dis-covered they could *choose* to love. Study 1 Corinthians 13:4-8, verses in the famous "love chapter." You will see that not one verse describes love in the emotional terms you might expect.

The good news is that once you choose to practice the Bi-ble's love principles, you also begin to experience emotional love.

Larry and Arlene found this principle to be true. They had been married for many years and had lost a sense of passion and romance by the time they saw me. When we first met, Arlene said she was considering divorce because Larry was like a roommate, not a husband. Yet as they learned to pray and talk together, they discovered a new depth of love that thrilled them both. It was a love based on living God's way instead of depending on human emotions.

Wendy also felt helpless in her marriage. Her husband Henry said he did not need help, so she came for counseling by herself. To her surprise, she learned there were many things she could do differently, including choosing to love Henry. As she expressed love, she was delighted to see Henry responding. Their marriage grew and flourished.

Nancy was deeply depressed at the thought of living with her husband Stu for the rest of her life. She too learned to choose to love her husband, but he never returned her love. Yet Nancy discovered a new joy and peace as she learned how to live in Christ's love. Although Stu divorced her a few years later, Nancy felt secure in the knowledge that she had truly loved him and had been obedient to God's Word.

"My mate doesn't love me."

It can be crushing to think you are unloved. Yet our love should not depend on being loved. Jesus said:

> *But I tell you: Love your enemies and pray for those who persecute you, that you may be sons of your Father in heaven. He causes his sun to rise on the evil and the good, and sends rain on the righteous and the unrighteous. (Matthew 5:44-45)*

Since Jesus said to love your enemy, you can be sure he wants you to love your mate, no matter what. Think about Christ's example. He loved those who rejected him.

How can you do this? Only with God's help. Sincerely ask him to help you follow the love instructions in 1 Corinthians 13, and you will see your attitude change. God will bless your obedience to his Word and, as time goes on, you will probably see your mate respond to your love.

"I'm so unhappy. This can't be what God wants."

Most people divorce because they are desperately unhappy. By disobeying God's Word and taking things into their own hands, they think they will find happiness. They pay a huge price. When they disobey God, they turn away from the source of joy—Jesus Christ.

> *If you obey my commands, you will remain in my love, just as I have obeyed my Father's commands and remain in his love. I have told you this so that my joy may be in you and that your joy may be complete. (John 15:11)*

If you think God doesn't want you to be miserable, you're right. However, he wants you to seek relief his way, not by sinning. The solution is to turn to the Lord and his Word—to learn how to experience his joy whatever your situation (Philippians 4:4 and James 1:2).

"We're incompatible," or, "We have grown apart."

You may think you and your spouse have incompatible personalities. Or you may not share similar beliefs, values, or interests. Perhaps your sex life is unsatisfying. Whatever the frustration, the answer is to learn how to flourish in your situation while working to improve it, not to run away.

Like many couples, Skeeter and I have extremely different personalities, talents, and interests. A small example of this would be our thoughts about butter and margarine. For many years I ate margarine, thinking it was healthier, and Skeeter ate butter, thinking it was tastier. We had many discussions, each trying to convince the other to switch. Our solution was to agree to disagree. We put a cube of each on the table. Then we both developed high cholesterol and began replacing the cubes with salsa.

Our vacation preferences provide another example. I dream of lying on a pink sand beach with warm, turquoise water lapping the shore. Skeeter yearns to explore museums and gardens. So we alternate between lying on beaches and visiting museums and gardens.

During more than three decades of marriage, we have had to accommodate hundreds of differences, large and small. As each of us has sought to learn from the other and to value our differences, we have both gained richer lives. I enjoy museums more than I once did, and Skeeter has come to love a good beach.

"I want to develop my ministry."

Harold longingly told me about the ministry he had with single adults before he married. He said that after marrying, he was so distracted by problems with his wife that he didn't have time for his ministry. He was sure God wanted him to divorce and move back into the ministry.

I hope you can see how foolish this argument was. Harold was saying he planned to disobey God so he could serve God.

"We were not married in God's eyes."

Some rationalize divorce by claiming they are not really married, saying, "All we have is a piece of paper." What a creative solution! Using the same logic, I could disavow any legal contract if I later decided God had not approved of it. My word and the authority of the law would no longer have a hold on me.

This obviously is not the way God looks at things. Remember the example of David and Bathsheba. There is no question that their marriage was not God's perfect plan, yet God did not have them divorce. Once you marry, you are married.

"He's not saved," or, "She's not a good Christian."

Even if your spouse is not a Christian, or is a lukewarm Christian, God says not to divorce. Instead, he calls on you to pray for your mate, be a great example, and win him or her to Christ through your love.

 If any brother has a wife who is not a believer and she is willing to live with him, he must not divorce her. And if a woman has a husband who is not a believer and he is willing to live with her, she must not divorce him. . . . How do you know, wife, whether you will save your husband? Or, how do you know, husband,

> *whether you will save your wife? (1 Corinthians 7:12-13, 16)*

> *Wives, in the same way be submissive to your husbands so that, if any of them do not believe the word, they may be won over without words by the behavior of their wives. (1 Peter 3:1)*

"I don't have peace."

Some justify divorce by saying, "I don't have peace, and God called me to peace." They are right when they say God wants them to experience peace. But they are wrong when they think they can get it by disobeying God's commands and seeking peace in their own fashion.

Imagine a harried mother telling her child, "I don't feel peace, so I'm leaving you and getting some nicer children." Or imagine a man in a lifeboat in the middle of the ocean saying, "I'm getting seasick" and jumping out of the boat. Divorcing your spouse to find peace is just as foolish—and just as serious an error in God's eyes.

Don't commit sin to find peace. Instead, seek God's peace in the midst of your circumstances. I love Jesus' words in the following passage:

> *In me you may have peace. In this world you will have trouble. But take heart! I have overcome the world. (John 16:33)*

"She would be happier without me."

Your mate may be unhappy, but don't use this as an excuse to divorce. You are not being noble or loving if you divorce. You simply are sinning.

The noblest thing you can do is obey God. Stay in your marriage, and work at making it the best one possible.

"We serve a forgiving God. He will forgive me."

The Bible *never* encourages us to sin while simultaneously claiming God's forgiveness. You can count on his forgiveness when you genuinely confess your sin, not when you harden your heart and disobey him.

God's Word is full of warnings about professing the name of the Lord while rejecting his commands. Read Malachi 2:13-14. God says that in spite of tears, weeping and wailing, he *"no longer pays attention to your offerings or accepts them with pleasure from your hands"* because of divorce.

"But," you might say, "We are living under grace. We serve a God of love. Don't be legalistic." Jude forcefully refuted this when he wrote that if you *"change the grace of our God into a license for immorality,"* you *"deny Jesus Christ our only Sovereign and Lord" (Jude 4)*. Paul also denounced this argument when he wrote:

 What shall we say, then? Shall we go on sinning so that grace may increase? By no means! We died to sin; how can we live in it any longer? (Romans 6:1-2)

When you divorce for non-scriptural reasons, you are actively rebelling against God. Study Hosea 7:13-14, 8:2-3, 9:4 and Amos 5:21 for warnings to those who claim to seek God but choose to sin at the same time.

No one is perfect (1 John 1:8). If we could not ask God's forgiveness, we would be without hope. But don't play games with the Lord by saying you love him while at the same time disobeying him.

"Divorce is no worse than other sins."

This excuse goes right along with, "We serve a forgiving God. He will forgive me." People who use this argument often have two points: (1) No sin is worse than other sins and (2) everybody sins from time to time, so what's the big deal?

If you think this way, you open the door to a world of sin, for you excuse it so easily. Consider Jack, an elder in his church who considered himself a good man. He was unhappy at home, so he left his wife to "have some time to think." As often happens at such times, he developed a relationship with another woman and eventually "fell in love."

Jack began lying to his wife, his friends, and his pastor. He became sexually active with the other woman and eventually left his church. He began attending another church and the lying grew. He now said his wife left him.

Jack began buying books about divorce and remarriage, desperately looking for justification to divorce. He no longer really cared about what God said. He just wanted an excuse. Paul's second letter to Timothy describes the man Jack had become:

> *For the time will come when men will not put up with sound doctrine. Instead, to suit their own desires, they will gather around them a great number of teachers to say what their itching ears want to hear. (2 Timothy 4:3)*

The argument that "divorce is no worse than other sins, so it's okay to divorce," is nonsense.

We should look for ways to please God, not excuses to disobey him. Read God's call to holiness in Leviticus 11:44, Romans 12:1, Ephesians 5:4-5, and 1 Thessalonians 4:7.

When you choose to sin, you put a distance between God and yourself. That distance grows because you have hardened your heart to his voice.

In some crucial aspects, it's not true that no sin is worse than other sins. Read Malachi 2:13-16 again to see the forcefulness of God's condemnation of divorce. Also read 1 Corinthians 6:13-20 in which Paul highlighted sexual sins because *"your body is a temple of the Holy Spirit" (1 Corinthians 6:19).*

"He is physically abusive."

There are situations in which you should take action to protect yourself. Physical abuse is one of them. A man cannot begin to understand the emotional harm, not to mention the physical damage, which he inflicts when he abuses his wife. The same is true with a physically abusive woman.

It is usually wise to separate when physical abuse occurs. The purpose of separating usually should not be to lay the foundation for a divorce, but rather to prevent further violence and provide adequate time for the couple to receive biblical counseling to build a solid marriage. (You will read more about this difficult topic later in this chapter in the section titled "Are there any other times God allows divorce?")

Other appropriate responses to abuse include talking to your pastor, calling the police, or getting a restraining order. It is okay for a Christian to appeal to the civil authorities. Read in Acts 25:11 about the time Saul claimed his rights as a Roman citizen when he was mistreated.

"I committed a sexual sin."

From time to time, I hear someone say, "Since I had an affair, our marriage is over and I'm free to divorce." That's not what the Bible says. If you committed adultery, your spouse may be free to divorce you, but it doesn't work the other way around.

"He committed mental adultery."

If your spouse longingly stares, or seems to stare, at someone else, don't say, "He looked at another woman lustfully. According to Matthew 5:27-28, he committed adultery in his heart, so I can divorce him." This would be a misuse of the Scriptures.

To use the same line of reasoning, I could take someone to court as a murderer for getting angry with me (Matthew 5:22 and 1 John 3:15). These passages are written to strengthen us against lust and anger, not to justify legal actions.

It hurts when your mate stares at others. Yet as you seek God and study, you will find grace and wisdom to deal with this trial.

There are hundreds of additional excuses.

The list of reasons people give for divorce is endless. For example: "He's an alcoholic." "She won't make love." "He's mean to my kids." "She smokes." "He's emotionally abusive." "She pushed me away." "I can't trust him." "God doesn't want me in an unhealthy relationship."

If you say such things, apply the scriptural principles discussed in the previous pages. Although you may face heartbreaking problems, they are not biblical reasons for divorce.

God loves you and will help you in your situation. Learn to *"cast all your anxiety on him because he cares for you" (1 Peter 5:7).* Trust him and follow his commands; he will help you through your hard times.

Make it personal ___ 🖉

Have you ever considered divorce for unscriptural reasons?
☐ Yes ☐ No

If you have considered divorce for unscriptural reasons, write the reasons, and then write what the Bible has to say about them.

Never Say, "Let's Divorce"

When you are broke you would never say, "Let's rob a bank." Along the same lines, when you are unhappy, do not say, "Let's divorce," "I don't see why we should stay married," or "You would be better off without me."

Not only should you never suggest divorce, you should resist even thinking about it. Harboring thoughts of divorce is like keeping chocolate chip cookies in the cookie jar when you are trying to diet. If the going gets tough, you can always eat a cookie—or bring up divorce.

Make it personal ___ ✐

Have you brought up the possibility of divorce, directly or indirectly? ☐ Yes ☐ No

Write a personal commitment not to do so in the future (unless you have scriptural grounds).

Tell your spouse that you are committed to him or her for life and that you will work to make your marriage better and better.

Check this box after you give your mate this message. ☐

Does God Ever Allow Divorce?

Although the Bible stresses the importance and permanence of marriage, it permits divorce in two different circumstances.

As you read the following, please remember that God sees you and your spouse as one flesh—and that he hates divorce. The reason I again am emphasizing this is that I have known *many* Christians who wanted out of their marriage and who looked intensely at the Scriptures to try to find an argument—any argument—for divorcing.

They weren't really seeking God's will. Instead, they were looking for a way to justify what they wanted to do. Please be careful not to approach the Word of God like that!

Divorce is allowed for sexual immorality.

Jesus said you may divorce if your spouse is sexually unfaithful. Notice, however, that he did not command you to divorce. He merely said it is permissible.

> *I tell you that anyone who divorces his wife, except for marital unfaithfulness, and marries another woman commits adultery. (Matthew 19:9)*

Re-read what I wrote earlier about "mental adultery." Jesus was talking about actual acts of sexual adultery, not looking, staring, or committing "mental adultery."

- **It usually is better to rebuild a marriage than divorce.**

  I have known many marriages in which the offender asked for forgiveness, the betrayed partner forgave, and the two successfully rebuilt their relationship. The process was painful and involved hard work, but the results were worth the effort. God was glorified, and these couples ended up with great marriages.

Ernie and Wilma are good examples. He had an affair and honestly repented. She forgave him, and then both came to counseling to rebuild their marriage on the Bible.

It was not an easy process for either. Wilma experienced devastating pain whenever she thought of the affair. Ernie learned to show understanding, sensitivity, and patience as he reaped the results of what he sowed (Galatians 6:7-8). Yet in the end they achieved a marriage filled with more joy and love than they had thought possible.

- **But—divorce for sexual immorality is permissible.**

It's usually best for a couple to rebuild their marriage if one spouse was sexually unfaithful. However, there may be exceptions—especially when one person continues in a pattern of unfaithfulness or is not willing to deal with his or her sin.

Joanna, a woman I counseled, was married for years to Hank, a leader in their church. He also was prominent in the larger Christian community. Over the years Hank had affairs with other women, most of whom attended their church. He continuously lied about his conduct, confessing only when Joanna confronted him with proof.

When cornered, Hank always said he was sorry, promised never to do it again, and asked for another chance. Joanna had a forgiving and compassionate heart and willingly forgave him. She also felt sympathy for the other women and often prayed for them.

This pattern continued for years. Each time it happened, Hank apologized but refused counseling or other help to rebuild the marriage. In fact, he got angry with Joanna for not trusting him after she forgave him.

Hank continued to sin sexually, refusing to do anything other than make false promises. Eventually, Joanna believed that God spoke to her heart and told her the marriage was over. With sadness, but feeling a great peace that she made the right choice, she divorced him.

Divorce is allowed if an unbeliever leaves.

If you are married to an unbeliever, it is God's desire for you to stay married. However, if your unbelieving spouse leaves, you are "not bound."

 To the rest I say this (I, not the Lord): If any brother has a wife who is not a believer and she is willing to live with him, he must not divorce her. And if a woman has a husband who is not a believer and he is willing to live with her, she must not divorce him. For the unbelieving husband has been sanctified through his wife, and the unbelieving wife has been sanctified through her believing husband. Otherwise your children would be unclean, but as it is, they are holy.

But if the unbeliever leaves, let him do so. A believing man or woman is not bound in such circumstances; God has called us to live in peace. How do you know, wife, whether you will save your husband? Or, how do you know, husband, whether you will save your wife? (1 Corinthians 7:12-16)

Is divorce permitted for "emotional desertion"?

Some think the previous verses justify divorce even if their spouse does not physically leave home. They state they are free to divorce if their mate has been unpleasant, financially irresponsible, sexually unavailable, or emotionally removed.

How do they come to such a conclusion? By saying that their spouse "left" or "deserted" them emotionally.

Such logic twists the clear meaning of the above passage, not to mention God's commands throughout the New Testament. Paul was writing about leaving physically. We all are married to imperfect spouses and at one time or another could justify divorce because of "emotional desertion." This reasoning is no better than saying that divorce is right if your spouse commits "mental adultery."

Is it ever okay to separate?

If you have marriage problems, it's usually best not to separate, but instead to stay together as you work them out. However, as I wrote earlier in this chapter, there may be exceptions (such as in the case of physical abuse) when it would be wise to physically separate. If you do move apart for a while, find a sound biblical counselor or pastor and begin the work of rebuilding your marriage.

Sometimes it may be wise to take the additional step of filing for legal separation. This might be appropriate, for example, if your spouse is a drug addict and is draining all the family finances. Talk with your pastor or a biblical counselor before taking this step.

Are there any other times God allows divorce?

The guidelines in this chapter cover the vast majority of situations I have encountered while counseling. However, there may be times when it's hard to know what to do.

For example, if your mate is put in prison for physically abusing you, this could qualify as a time when divorce is permissible since your unbelieving spouse physically left you.

If you are unsure about your circumstances, talk with a wise pastor or counselor. Look for someone who is committed to helping you discover and apply the Bible's truths, not someone whose basic philosophy is, "God doesn't want you to be unhappy, so if you're unhappy, divorce."

What if You Already Have Divorced?

If you divorced for unbiblical reasons, particularly if you were a Christian when you did so, you need to face the seriousness of your sin. Do not pretend that divorcing your spouse was not sinful or that it somehow was okay with God. It was not.

I am extremely concerned for Christians who divorce and remarry for unscriptural reasons and are not willing to face their sin. When we choose to sin, we harden our hearts toward God and his commandments. Then rather than genuinely confessing, we justify our actions. People say, for example, "I know it was a sin, but it was the only thing I could do." Or, "We live under grace, not law." Or, "I knew it was wrong, but Jesus told me he would forgive me if I did it."

Nonsense. It was not Jesus who told them it was okay to divorce. He commanded us not to divorce and added that if we divorce for unscriptural reasons and remarry, we commit adultery (Matthew 19:9).

The Bible uses stinging words to describe those who justify sin by saying "We live under grace." Here's how they are described in the book of Jude:

> *They are godless men, who change the grace of our God into a license for immorality and deny Jesus Christ our only Sovereign and Lord. (Jude 4)*

Walt said he knew the Bible condemns divorce, but planned to divorce Shelly anyway because "God is a forgiving God." Shelly protested the divorce and wrote letters pleading for another chance. His response, even as he went through the divorce proceedings, was to give her angry speeches, saying she must forgive him because she was a Christian. He divorced her, married another woman, and now attends church as if nothing happened.

Margaret told her husband Richard she intended to divorce him and then marry a man who was divorcing his wife. She said they planned to approach their church and ask forgiveness after they married. She clearly was playing games with God and choosing to rebel against his Word. Her planned "repentance" was a sham.

I could go on and on describing people's rationalizations for divorce. For example, some say, "After I divorce and marry someone else, we will commit adultery the first time we have sex. After that it won't be adultery."

Those who justify sin will not be so nonchalant when they stand before God in judgment. He is not impressed by our excuses.

 For we must all appear before the judgment seat of Christ, that each one may receive what is due him for the things done while in the body, whether good or bad. (2 Corinthians 5:10)

If you divorced your spouse for unscriptural reasons and you both are Christians, you probably should pursue restoration of your marriage if neither of you has remarried. However, seek counsel from a Bible-believing pastor before you make a decision. There are many possible complications that fall outside the confines of this book.

If you were a Christian when you divorced and have married someone else, confess that you started in sin. If you truly confess, Christ will forgive you (1 John 1:9) and help you deal with the mess you created. By truly confess, I mean to (1) genuinely face the sinfulness of divorcing and (2) acknowledge that if you could make the decision again, you would not divorce. Anything else would be half-hearted and come short of genuine confession.

After confessing your sin, do not divorce your present spouse to remarry your previous mate. You cannot undo the effect of sin by sinning again.

There is hope in the Lord, even in this ungodly situation. When we disobey God's Word, we suffer. But when we honestly and humbly confess our sins, Christ helps us put the past behind and press on. As Paul wrote:

 Forgetting what is behind, and straining toward what is ahead, I press on toward the goal to win the prize for which God called me heavenward in Christ Jesus. (Philippians 3:13-14)

However, do not be nonchalant about *"forgetting what is behind."* You have harmed others and need to do what you can to promote healing. At the least, you probably should apologize to your ex-spouse, children, close friends, and church. When you offer an apology, do not make excuses. Be sure to respond with understanding, patience, and love if others do not forgive you.

Let me close this section by offering the example of Skeeter and myself as an encouragement. As I previously wrote, we married because she became pregnant. We clearly started our marriage in a bad way and suffered many unpleasant consequences. However, we eventually turned to God and confessed our sins. Although we had to deal with the consequences, we also experienced the grace of God and have enjoyed an ever-growing and deeply satisfying marriage. When you genuinely confess your sins, God can build mansions out of ashes.

Make it personal ___ 🖋

If you divorced for unscriptural reasons, are you willing to face your sin, truly confess, and ask God's forgiveness? ☐ Yes ☐ No

What steps do you need to take? Is there anyone to whom you should apologize?

_____

There is Hope in the Lord

This chapter was written with one goal—to encourage you to truly commit to your marriage. Even if you think you are stuck with a miserable marriage for the rest of your life, take heart. God loves you and wants the best for you. His commands are for your good.

As you read this book and the following books in this series, you will discover principles to help you live with satisfaction and joy regardless of your situation. You also will learn many ways to transform an unsatisfying marriage into a great one.

Many people say divorce brings freedom. That is no more true than the serpent's promises to Eve in the Garden of Eden (Genesis 3:1-5). Living according to God's Word provides *true* freedom—the freedom of a clean conscience, freedom from the tyranny and consequences of sin and freedom to enjoy God's love.

Putting It All Together — Chapter 4

Key point: Never entertain or bring up the possibility of divorce.

Memory verse: *"Therefore what God has joined together, let man not separate." (Matthew 19:6)*

Action plan: Choose one or two lessons from this chapter to work on this week:

1.

2.

Chapter 5
Forgive Your Spouse

Forgive whatever grievances you may have against one another. Forgive as the Lord forgave you. (Colossians 3:13)

Several years ago, Ellen, an extremely agitated woman, came in for an initial counseling session. Her stomach jerked in enormous, nervous convulsions, and her words tumbled out in spurts. She said she had a desperate problem and could see no way out except suicide. She had a gun at home and planned to kill herself.

What was the problem? In the past, Ellen had been a compulsive shopper and put her family deeply in debt. Her husband George had threatened to divorce her if it ever happened again. For some time she avoided any problems, but then she again started spending beyond their income.

This time Ellen had spent much more than before. Although she had hidden their enormous debts from George, she knew the cover-up could not last much longer. She had not made a payment on their home mortgage for several months and had thrown away all the bank's warning letters. She came to see me after learning the bank had started foreclosure. She was panicked because her husband would know everything in a few days.

As we talked, she began to calm down as she realized things were not hopeless. I telephoned George and made plans to talk with him alone the next day, and then to talk with both of them together. When George and I met, I told him about their financial catastrophe, Ellen's fear that he would divorce her, and her talk of suicide.

Then we talked about his shortcomings, how he had contributed to her spending. When Ellen joined us in the office later, George wholeheartedly forgave her spending and asked forgiveness for his faults. Her relief was obvious. Over the next few weeks, she became increasingly relaxed as they engaged in many frank discussions about their marriage. His willingness to forgive may have saved her life. This same willingness to forgive has opened the door to rebuilding countless marriages over the years. I have seen people forgive sexual affairs, lack of attention, pornography, drunkenness, physical abuse, dishonesty, gambling, laziness, irresponsibility, and practically anything else you could think of. Forgiveness often was the balm that allowed the marriage to begin to heal.

You too may need to forgive your spouse for serious transgressions. And you certainly will need to forgive everyday irritations such as carelessness, forgetfulness and habits that annoy you.

A few years ago, I read in the newspaper about a house in which nobody removed the trash for years. The rooms were filled with garbage. Little paths ran between the piles. Rats were everywhere. The stench was awful, and the rottenness worked its way into the floors and walls until they had to bulldoze the house.

Not forgiving is like not taking out the garbage. It can rot the walls and floors of your marriage.

Forgiveness is God's way of keeping our hearts clean to love each other. Forgiveness is a way of life in a great marriage.

Make it personal ___ 🖉

Do you sometimes have trouble forgiving your spouse?
☐ Yes ☐ No

Ask your spouse if he or she thinks you are forgiving or if you seem to hold grudges. Write the answer here.

Forgive in Obedience to God

If you are like most people, you sometimes hang on to hurts, thinking you have a right to be angry. In fact, you might be upset if someone suggests forgiving your spouse, given what your mate did to you. But we are told throughout the Bible to forgive. Since God tells us to forgive, we must forgive.

 Be kind and compassionate to one another, forgiving each other, just as Christ forgave you. (Ephesians 4:32)

Bear with each other and forgive whatever grievances you may have against one another. Forgive as the Lord forgave you. (Colossians 3:13)

Follow Jesus' example in forgiveness.

When Jesus died on the cross and then rose from the dead, he took all our sins upon himself and offered us new lives. You and I should follow his example and extend the same grace to others.

Forgive even if your spouse does not apologize.

You may think that unless your mate says "I'm sorry," you are not required to forgive. But we must always forgive, even if the other person insists he or she did nothing wrong.

Jesus forgave his executioners as he died on the cross, in spite of the fact that they did not apologize (Luke 23:34). Likewise, Stephen said, *"Lord, do not hold this sin against them"* as he was stoned to death (Acts 7:60).

Forgive even if your mate's apology seems fake.

Have you ever said, "'I'm sorry' doesn't cut it"? You may withhold forgiveness because you think your spouse's apology is insincere. Or you may think your mate did not apologize "correctly." For example, you might find it hard to forgive if your spouse says, "I'm sorry if your feelings were hurt" instead of confessing to actually doing something wrong.

It is not your job to judge the sincerity of an apology. Your mate's genuineness is between him or her and God. Your only responsibility is to forgive.

Realize God forgives us just as we forgive others.

Jesus could have given no stronger message about forgiveness than when he said God will not forgive us if we do not forgive others.

> *For if you forgive men when they sin against you, your heavenly Father will also forgive you. But if you do not forgive men their sins, your Father will not forgive your sins. (Matthew 6:14-15)*

Study the story of the unmerciful servant in Matthew 18:23-35. In this parable, Jesus taught about a king who canceled a huge debt his servant owed him. The servant then turned around and threw another servant in prison because this man owed him a small sum of money.

When the king learned about the first servant's actions, he punished him severely and said, *"Shouldn't you have had mercy on your fellow servant just as I had on you?" (Matthew 18:33).*

Make it personal ___ 🖉

Do you harbor unforgiveness in your heart? ☐ Yes ☐ No

If you have held on to bitterness, write a prayer asking God to forgive you and to help you change your attitude.

Have you ever withheld forgiveness because your mate did not apologize or because his or her apology seemed insincere?
☐ Yes ☐ No

How will you remind yourself to forgive even if your spouse doesn't apologize or seems insincere?

Forgive to Bring Healing

Forgiveness is a great and sometimes costly gift that can bring healing in your marriage. When you forgive, you may think you are giving up your "right" to be angry. What you really are doing is giving up the "right" to be unhappy and have an awful marriage.

I know one woman who lived with bitterness for forty years because her husband flirted with her sister early in their marriage. What was the result? Forty years of unhappiness and a miserable marriage.

When you do not forgive your spouse, bitterness festers within you, growing and spreading like cancer. The Bible warns, *"See to it that no one misses the grace of God and that no bitter root grows up" (Hebrews 12:15).*

You may say, "My spouse doesn't deserve forgiveness. He would get off too easily." Or, "I suffered, so now she's going to suffer." Although your lack of forgiveness may wound your spouse, it probably hurts you even more. When you forgive, it releases you from self-pity and helps you experience God's peace.

When I was a child and went on backpacking trips, I loved the sensation of lightness I felt when I took off a pack I had carried for hours. When we forgive, we can experience that same heady sensation of lightness.

Make it personal ___ 🖋

Describe one time you experienced bitterness and resentment because you did not forgive.

Now describe a time when you experienced peace because you forgave.

Choose to Forgive

Many think of forgiveness as something you either *feel* or you don't. But forgiveness is an act of the will, a choice. It is a decision, not an emotion.

Choose to forgive in obedience to Christ. God will change your emotions over time.

Ask God's help.

Some things are hard to forgive. It is human nature to resist letting someone off the hook. Ask the Lord to help you.

Forgive quickly.

Forgive as soon as you can. When you hold on to an offense, you give it life and strength, making it harder to forgive in the long run. As one of my friends put it, "If I don't let go fast, it starts tasting good when I lick it."

Sometimes forgive silently.

There will be times when you and your spouse talk about a problem such as a bounced check and you openly forgive him or her. However, as you go through life there are numerous times when it is gracious to forgive silently. For example, there's no need to point it out every time your mate forgets to pick up dirty clothes, is late, or runs out of gas. The Bible says, *"Love each other deeply, because love covers over a multitude of sins" (1 Peter 4:8).*

Make it personal _____ 🖉

Have you thought forgiveness was an emotion? ☐ Yes ☐ No

What is an example of something else (other than forgiving) you choose to do because it's the right thing, whether or not you feel like doing it?

Forgive with a Humble Attitude

If you need to forgive your spouse, seek God's help to maintain the right attitude, watching out for self-righteousness. One thing that helps me do this when I'm upset with Skeeter is to remember all my failures. Then it is hard to be amazed or mad at her shortcomings.

Have you ever said, "Sure I sin, but I would never do what my spouse did"? Be careful. When you say this, you are making the assumption that God sees your sins as less serious than your spouse's. You could be wrong.

Ask yourself if you are partially responsible. Recognize that your actions may have contributed to your mate's failures. Do not accept the blame for your spouse's sins, but be willing to examine any role you might have played. At the beginning of this chapter, I wrote about Ellen, a woman who spent money compulsively. As I counseled her and her husband, it became obvious that he had neglected her for years, often working extremely long hours and then coming home and settling down in front of the television. One reason she spent all that money was that she felt neglected.

Did this excuse Ellen's sins? No. Yet George needed to acknowledge that he had contributed to her problem and confess his sins.

Realize it may take time for pain to heal. Early in our marriage we owned a dog, Sandy, whom I loved. Over the years we have had several other dogs, but I never felt the wonderful closeness with them that I did with Sandy.

One weekend I flew out of state to interview for a job. While I was gone, Skeeter went camping with our son and left Sandy at home with plenty of food and water. We have no idea what happened to Sandy, but we never saw her again.

The pain I felt at her loss was indescribable. I wanted to be mad at Skeeter, but knew I had to forgive her. Realizing that I too would have left Sandy alone for a day helped, but only a little. By the grace of God, I forgave Skeeter and truly determined not to hold anything against her.

The pain subsided and eventually went away, but over the next two decades it periodically rose up. Seemingly out of nowhere it would sweep over me. Did that mean I had not forgiven Skeeter? No, it simply meant that I was a human being who loved his dog.

Is there a Sandy in your life? Do not despair if you find yourself upset over something you thought you had forgiven. Instead of wondering if you really forgave in the first place, simply reaffirm your decision to forgive. Pray for the grace of God to be more firmly entrenched in your heart.

The pain in your life may come from something more serious than a lost dog. If your spouse admits to having had an affair, don't feel guilty if you do not immediately feel forgiveness. Decide to forgive your spouse, but also realize that it may take time for severe emotional wounds to heal.

Allow your spouse to rebuild trust.

Ask God's help to be aware of things your mate does to rebuild trust. Acknowledge them.

Make it personal ___ ✐

Which of the above points will help you forgive? How will they help?

Overcome Your Objections to Forgiving

The following are common statements voiced by people who have trouble forgiving. Check any you have said or thought.

☐　**"I could forgive anything except lying."**
　　We sometimes define our own "unpardonable sin." A common example is, "I could forgive anything except lying. If I can't trust my spouse, we don't have a real marriage." Living with dishonesty is unpleasant, but God's Word does not make lying an exception. We are to forgive.

☐　**"My spouse keeps making the same mistake."**
　　You may say, "I would be willing to forgive if I saw genuine sorrow and an effort to change, but my spouse keeps doing the same thing over and over." Jesus told us what to do about repeated sins: Keep forgiving.

 Then Peter came to Jesus and asked, "Lord, how many times shall I forgive my brother when he sins against me? Up to seven times?" Jesus answered, "I tell you, not seven times, but seventy-seven ["seventy times seven" in the King James Bible] times." (Matthew 18:21-22)

Don't keep score. As Paul wrote, love *"keeps no record of wrongs" (1 Corinthians 13:5).* Two practical guidelines are:

- **Do not dwell on the offense.**
　　You can control your thoughts. Choose to think about things that are pure and praiseworthy (Philippians 4:8).

- **Do not bring it up to your spouse or others.**
  Once you forgive your spouse's behavior, do not throw it in your mate's face or gossip about it with others.

☐ **"I don't want to excuse the sin."**
Many people think if they forgive they are giving their mate the message that he or she didn't do anything wrong. That's not the case at all. You simply are forgiving.

☐ **"She hurt me, and I want her to suffer."**
You may have suffered grievous wounds and desire revenge, but Jesus said to love your enemies (Matthew 5:44) and to forgive others (Matthew 6:12). Study Matthew 5:44, 1 Thessalonians 5:15, and 1 Peter 3:9 to understand the attitude you should have in the face of mistreatment. Leave vengeance, if any, to God (Psalm 94:1 and Romans 12:19).

☐ **"I can't forget. I guess I haven't forgiven him."**
Some people think you have not forgiven unless you have literally forgotten a transgression. It's true that God sometimes removes the memory of offenses. However, even if we have forgiven we probably will remember some events for a long time.

Suppose, for example, that your spouse burned your house down last month. Although you forgave him or her, it's unlikely you ever will forget who set the fire. But despite your memories, you can change the way you remember the fire and no longer hold it against your mate.

Let me add one more thought about "forgetting." If you hear yourself saying, "I can forgive, but I can't forget," examine your heart. What you really might be saying is, "I don't forgive you."

☐ **"I get tired of my spouse always apologizing."**
If you are married to someone who frequently says "I'm sorry" for different things throughout the day, he

or she may be insecure in your love or acceptance. Instead of responding with annoyance, reassure your spouse of your love. Explain that constantly apologizing for little things is not necessary. Look for ways to show love in your actions and words throughout the day.

Make it personal ___ 🖋

Have you had trouble forgiving because of any of these objections? ☐ Yes ☐ No

If so, write a prayer asking God help you overcome your objections.

Forgive, Yet also Deal with Issues

God expects you to forgive, yet that doesn't mean you never should talk about problems. And it doesn't always mean dropping an issue after granting forgiveness. At times it may be wise to take further steps, from talking over what happened to protecting yourself.

Sometimes gently express your feelings.

Love sometimes requires gentle confrontation in addition to forgiveness. But the "confrontation" always should be done courteously (Galatians 6:1).

When Molly and Fred met with me, she was hurt and frustrated. It seemed to her that one of Fred's favorite activities was to make fun of her when they were with friends. He thought his jokes were hilarious, but she was deeply wounded and alternated between silent suffering and screaming.

Although it often is appropriate to quietly forgive without saying anything, at other times the most loving thing to do is to gently speak up. As the Bible says, *"Better is open rebuke than hidden love" (Proverbs 27:5)*. Sometimes it is good to quietly say, "That hurt me" or, "I think you owe me an apology." Molly needed to forgive, but she also needed to learn the art of gentle confrontation.

Talk together after forgiving.

Further discussion often helps a couple learn from a problem or make a decision. For example, after you forgive your spouse for forgetting a dinner date, it may be a good idea to gently explain how you felt about being forgotten and then make another date.

Remember that you have forgiven your mate. Talk as a friend, not as someone rubbing salt in a wound.

Learn from the past.

Although you must not hold a grudge, you may need to learn from the past and use wisdom as you look to the future. If limits seem necessary, make them as a team if possible. For example, Ellen and George both agreed that since Ellen had trouble controlling spending, she no longer would carry credit cards.

Take protective action when appropriate.

You must always forgive, yet there are times when it is wise and loving also to take strong action. You can forgive your mate for physical abuse, yet still call the police or move out. If your spouse commits sexual immorality, it may be appropriate to file for divorce (although, as I wrote in Chapter 4, it's usually best to rebuild your marriage).

Make it personal ___ 🖉

Do you need to take any of the above steps in addition to forgiving? ☐ Yes ☐ No

If so, what will you do?

Practice Forgiveness

Now that you have studied forgiveness, it's time to forgive anything you hold against your mate. Do not take this step lightly. Spend time in prayer to identify any poison that may be festering in your heart.

If you are not sure if you are harboring unforgiveness, ask yourself the following questions. If you check "yes" to any of them, it's a sign there may be areas you need to forgive.

☐ Do you dwell on your mate's shortcomings or sins?

☐ Do you talk about them with others?

- [ ] Do you feel anger, resentment or bitterness?
- [ ] Are you upset at what your spouse gets away with?
- [ ] Do you hope bad things will happen to your mate?
- [ ] Do you feel sorry for yourself?

Make it personal ___ ✐

Do you hold anything in your heart against your spouse? (Ask God to show you if there is anything before you answer.)
☐ Yes ☐ No

Talk to God: *"Lord, in Jesus' name I forgive my mate for [name everything you need to forgive]. Please forgive me for holding on to a grudge and please help me continue to walk in forgiveness."*
Check this box after you pray. ☐

Talk with your spouse: If your spouse has been aware of your unforgiveness, tell him or her, "I forgive you. I'm sorry for holding on to a grudge. Please forgive me for my attitude."
Check this box after you talk with your spouse. ☐

Putting It All Together — Chapter 5

Key point: Choose to forgive your spouse for his or her shortcomings and sins.

Memory verse: *"Forgive whatever grievances you may have against one another. Forgive as the Lord forgave you."* *(Colossians 3:13)*

Action plan: Choose one or two lessons from this chapter to work on this week:

1.

2.

Chapter 6
Ask Forgiveness

If you ... remember that your brother has something against you ... go and be reconciled. (Matthew 5:23-24)

Imagine that last week your spouse asked you never to make plans for the two of you without first talking together. You thought that sounded reasonable and agreed, but this afternoon you forgot and invited a couple over for dinner tomorrow night. Now you are headed home after work, worried about how your mate will react when you announce the dinner invitation.

If your spouse were to explode with anger when you mention it, how do you think you would respond?

☐ I would react with anger.

☐ I would complain about always being criticized and never being appreciated.

☐ I would counterattack, pointing out things my mate failed to do.

☐ I would feel like a loser who never does anything right.

☐ I would say, "It's no big deal. I just forgot."

☐ I would scold my spouse for not being hospitable.

☐ I would say nothing, withdraw and pout.

☐ I would apologize and ask forgiveness.

In Chapter 5, we looked at the importance of forgiving when our spouse disappoints us. In this chapter, we will look at another aspect of forgiveness—asking forgiveness when *we* do something wrong.

Most of us are amateurs at asking forgiveness, whether for a relatively light thing such as forgetting to buy something at the store or for a more serious offense such as gambling away the grocery money.

Why is this? The most common reason is pride. Another is the fear that if you ask forgiveness, you let down your emotional defenses and open yourself up to further attacks.

When you ask forgiveness, you may feel like a groveling slave squirming on the floor before an angry master. God looks at it differently. He sees you as being both humble and strong in his Spirit.

 For everyone who exalts himself will be humbled, and he who humbles himself will be exalted. (Luke 14:11)

Apologizing brings healing.

Apologizing for your shortcomings or sins is like applying oil to a squeaky hinge. It makes your marriage work much more smoothly. On the other hand, if you don't apologize, the hinge may squeak louder and louder until it drowns out all other sounds.

Asking forgiveness brings peace. It makes it easier for your mate to forgive you and sets the stage for rebuilding trust between you.

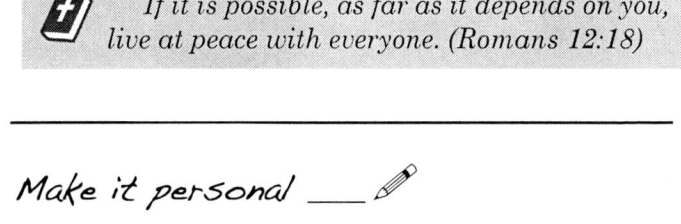 *If it is possible, as far as it depends on you, live at peace with everyone. (Romans 12:18)*

Make it personal ___ 🖉

Do you need to ask forgiveness more often? ☐ Yes ☐ No

Do you find it difficult to ask forgiveness? If so, why?

First Ask God's Forgiveness

When you sinned against your spouse, you also sinned against God. Before you do anything else, ask God to forgive you. You can count on his forgiveness when you genuinely confess.

 If we confess our sins, he is faithful and just and will forgive us our sins and purify us from all unrighteousness. (1 John 1:9)

Don't say, "I know God forgives me, but I can't forgive myself." That would be refusing a wonderful gift God offers you. When God forgives you, you are forgiven. Accept it with thankfulness.

Make it personal ___ ✎

Read Ezekiel 18:23 and 32, Luke 23:34, and 1 John 1:9. Write the lessons you learn from these verses.

If you have trouble accepting God's forgiveness, write one of the above verses in this space. Memorize it, and then meditate on it when you feel guilty.

Pray for a humble attitude.

God wants us to humble ourselves before one another (1 Peter 5:5). Instead, we often argue about who caused a problem or who started an argument. Rather than approaching each other as friends, we act like opposing attorneys in a courtroom.

Humble people are not afraid to admit a mistake because they are sure of God's love and acceptance. They know they are not perfect (James 3:2) and do not mind if others know it. Yet they do not think that by apologizing they are shouldering all the blame for the problem. They are able to say "I'm sorry" without groveling. They know that apologizing is God's way to restore peace.

> *Clothe yourselves with humility toward one another, because, "God opposes the proud but gives grace to the humble." (1 Peter 5:5)*

Make it personal ____ 🖋

Write a prayer asking God for a humble attitude. Also ask him to help you apologize in a manner that will be easy for your spouse to accept.

Apologize

Apologizing means saying "I'm sorry," but it also means much more. The following suggestions will help you apologize successfully and bring healing to your marriage.

Identify how you offended your spouse.

If your mate is upset and you aren't sure why, sometimes it is best not to immediately ask what the problem is. Your offense may be so obvious that your spouse will be offended if you don't see it on your own. Spend quiet time with God, asking him to help you accurately see your attitudes and actions.

If after praying you still are unsure what happened, don't say, "Is something wrong?" Ask, instead, "Have I done something wrong?" By asking if you have done something wrong, you are humbling yourself and making it easier for your mate to respond.

Or you could say something like, "It's easy to see I've blown it, but I don't understand how. I apologize for being so insensitive. Please help me understand what I did wrong, so I can learn for the future." If your spouse answers, listen. If he or she is angry, thinking you ought to know, be understanding.

If your mate voices a complaint and you don't agree with him or her, do not react immediately. Instead, try to see things through his or her eyes. Pray for wisdom. It may be that you are blind to your faults.

Even if your spouse exaggerates, there may be some truth to the complaint. Carefully consider his or her words. You usually can find ways in which you contributed to a problem. For example, although you may think your position was correct in an argument, you may have spoken angry words and need to apologize.

Approach your spouse before he or she complains.

Don't wait for your husband or wife to bring up your mistakes before apologizing. Ask God to help you be aware of when you say or do something wrong. Then say "I'm sorry" before your mate says anything.

Say, "I'm sorry."

Giving flowers or making some other gesture can help communicate your remorse, but be sure to give a clear message by saying you are sorry. If you don't, your spouse may be confused about what your actions mean. He or she could think the flowers mean, "I didn't do anything wrong, but let's have peace."

- **Be specific.**

  Do not merely say, "I'm sorry for the problem," or, "I'm sorry you are unhappy." Say exactly what you did wrong. For example, "I'm sorry I overdrew the checking account."

- **Use words that your mate finds easy to accept.**

  Some people have a preference for specific words to be used in an apology. Perhaps your spouse does not like "I apologize" and prefers, instead, "I'm sorry." If your husband or wife has a preference, be sure to act on it.

Allow your spouse to talk.

If your mate complains about something you said or did, apologize as soon as possible. However, it's usually wisest not to interrupt while your spouse is talking. If you break in too soon, he or she may be frustrated, thinking you don't really understand how much your actions hurt.

Apologize even if your husband or wife is angry.

One of the hardest times to apologize for most of us is when our mate is critical, angry, bitter, or sarcastic. We usually react defensively instead of focusing on our own problems.

Remember the Bible's instructions in 1 Peter 3:9: *"Do not repay evil with evil, or insult with insult, but with blessing."* Humble yourself and apologize, even if your spouse does not make it easy for you.

Apologize although you didn't mean to offend.

There may be times when you unintentionally hurt your spouse. If this happens, be gracious and apologize. If you find yourself getting upset at your mate's reaction, ask God for a spirit of humility and grace before you speak.

For example, if you break your husband's or wife's favorite dish, say you're sorry. Likewise, if you bought your spouse a purple shirt as a present and the response was, "You know I hate purple," apologize without being defensive.

Go light on rationalizations.

Has your spouse ever been upset at you when you were trying to do the right thing? Perhaps you tried to give a compliment, but your mate misinterpreted your words. Or maybe you came home later than you said you would because of an unexpected problem at work.

It usually does not undermine your apology if you give a valid explanation after you say, "I'm sorry." But be careful. Many people frequently make excuses and rarely apologize. If you are late again and again, your explanations become less meaningful. Even if you have a good excuse for being late this time, your track record may be bad. Apologize and make a commitment to change your habits.

Apologize even if your spouse also was at fault.

Don't argue over who was most at fault. Say you are sorry for what you did wrong, even if you think you are almost completely right and your spouse is almost completely wrong. (Although you think you are only one percent wrong, God may see it differently!)

Do not turn an apology into an accusation.

Be careful not to point out your spouse's faults when you apologize. For example, don't say, "I'm sorry for the one percent I was wrong," or "I'm sorry I got angry when you were so mean." Such comments are not apologies but invitations to argue.

Simply apologize for what you did wrong. Say, "I'm deeply sorry for the way I talked. Will you forgive me?"

I hesitate to say there are exceptions to this principle because so many of us look for excuses to lash back. However, there are exceptions. For example, if your mate hit you because you burned the toast, it would not be smart to apologize for burning the toast. It would be much more appropriate, instead, to take strong actions such as calling your pastor or the police. Although there may be times when loving confrontation is more appropriate than apologizing, remember that simply apologizing is called for in the vast majority of cases.

Never offer a deal.
You may be tempted to say, "I'll forgive you if you forgive me." Don't do that. God wants you to apologize whether or not your mate does.

Discuss it if your spouse constantly criticizes you.
If your mate seems to constantly criticize you or demand apologies, you may become discouraged and beaten down. Or you may fight back, fearing that to continually apologize would encourage more criticism.

It is appropriate to gently discuss your frustration if you find yourself in this situation. Explain that you want to be responsive to your spouse's desires, but you are overwhelmed by all the criticism.

Even if your spouse doesn't respond well to this discussion, do not accept his or her opinion that you are a bad person. Instead, be comforted by the knowledge that God loves you. Pray for your mate, knowing that he or she has a critical spirit.

Respond humbly if you think you were not at fault.
If you carefully listen to your spouse's complaints and pray for understanding, but still are sure you are 100 percent faultless, do not dishonestly accept blame. Say something like, "I'm really sorry for causing you distress, but I'm having trouble seeing that what I did was wrong. I know I could be blind to my faults. I'll keep praying and will seek God's help to see clearly." Then keep praying. It is unlikely you are completely faultless.

A different response is in order if your mate makes a false accusation, such as "I know you're seeing someone else." Realize that your spouse is insecure. Do not react with anger or get into an argument. Gently and lovingly offer reassurance of your love.

Make it personal ___ 🖉

In light of the above guidelines, do you need to change the way you apologize? ☐ Yes ☐ No

If so, what changes will you make in how you apologize?

Ask your spouse to evaluate how often and how well you apologize. Write his or her suggestions here.

Ask for Forgiveness

Follow up your apology by asking, "Will you forgive me?" There is real power in these four words. If you don't ask for forgiveness, tension can hang in the air after you apologize. Once you ask forgiveness and your spouse answers "yes," the tension usually begins to fade away.

Make it personal ____ ✐

Do you usually ask for forgiveness after apologizing?
☐ Yes ☐ No

Why is it a good idea to ask for forgiveness?

Deal with Past Sins

I have been writing about how to deal with wrongs as they come up. But what if you have a backlog of offenses you committed against your mate for which you have never apologized? Now is a good time to wipe the slate clean. Take some time to quiet yourself before God, and ask him to show you any unconfessed past sins.

You may be surprised by what comes to mind. You may think of specific incidents. Or you might think of an ongoing problem, such as often getting angry.

Asking forgiveness for past wrongs can heal old wounds and give your relationship a fresh start. Perhaps you were sexually active as a couple before you married. Either or both of you may have a lingering sense of guilt, or a sense that sex is sinful, because of that experience. Asking forgiveness can be a first step toward healing your sexual relationship.

Make it personal ___ 🖉

Ask God to show you any sins for which you need to apologize. Write them here, along with plans to apologize.

Answer Unforgiveness with Love

Let's say you forgot your spouse's birthday and said, "I'm sorry. Please forgive me." How would you respond if your mate reacted to your apology with rage or by saying, "I don't believe you"? Check each response you might make:

☐ I would say, "If that's the way you feel, I'm not sorry."

☐ I would say, "And you call yourself a Christian? What a phony!"

☐ I would say, "If that's what you think, I don't see why we should stay married."

☐ I would silently withdraw, feeling sorry for myself.

☐ I would stomp away in anger.

☐ I would say, "I understand your anger. I hope you can forgive me later."

When your mate does not react to your apology with "I forgive you," you have a chance to show how sorry you really are. If you respond, "In that case, I'm not sorry," you prove your apology was phony. If you were truly sorry, you still would be sorry. Be prepared to say "I'm sorry" more than once for the same offense.

One thing you should *not* do is give your spouse a speech about how Christians are supposed to forgive.

The following are ways to deal with three common responses you might face after apologizing:

Your spouse says, "It's hard to forgive."

Your mate may say, "I want to forgive you, but it's going to take time." If he or she says that, accept it graciously. Do not push for a statement of complete forgiveness.

Your spouse does not believe you are sincere.

If your mate says, "I don't believe you mean it," search your heart to see if you really are sorry. It's possible your words were insincere.

On the other hand, your words may have been honest. In that case say, "I really am sorry and I hope you will come to believe me." Do not get into an argument. Let your attitude and actions prove your sincerity.

Your spouse is angry or says, "I won't forgive you."

If your mate reacts in anger and refuses to forgive you, say something such as, "I understand I hurt you and hope you can forgive me sometime." Silently forgive your spouse for not forgiving you.

Let's look at Jerry and his wife Donna to see this principle in action. Jerry spoke harshly to Donna one morning and left home in a foul mood. As he drove to work, the Lord showed him that he needed to apologize.

Jerry rehearsed his apology throughout the day and imagined Donna smiling in appreciation as he spoke, forgiving him and giving him a big hug.

When he came home, she greeted him with a glare. Holding fast to his plan, he said he was sorry for his angry words and asked forgiveness. Donna ignored his words and chewed him out for being so mean.

How would you advise Jerry to respond? A better question might be, how would you respond if your spouse reacted to your apology that way?

The best response would be to wait quietly and then say, "I understand your anger. I'm really sorry and hope you will forgive me." If you are sorry, you should be willing to listen to a short, angry speech. You helped stir up the anger and should be ready to suffer some consequences.

If your spouse's speech goes on for more than a few minutes, ask yourself if you apologized humbly and fully or if you were half-hearted. Reassure your mate that you are indeed sorry.

If the tirade continues and you find yourself getting upset, it may be wise to say, "I'm really sorry for the way I acted, but I'm not handling this very well. I need to call 'time-out.' Let's talk later."

However, if you have done something very serious, such as committing a sexual sin, the wisest, fairest, and most loving thing to do might be to continue to listen to your spouse. By doing so, you would acknowledge the suffering you caused, demonstrate your sorrow, and show a desire to rebuild your relationship.

Make it personal _____ 🖉

How will you respond if your mate reacts poorly to an apology?

Rebuild Trust

I still remember Terrence sitting in my office and telling his wife Kelly, "Sure, I committed adultery last night, but I refuse to dwell in the past. You must forgive me and never bring it up again because you are a Christian." His attitude demonstrated profound immaturity and lack of understanding.

If you committed a serious offense, such as having an affair or hitting your mate, it is as if you stepped on a kitten and broke its leg. Your job is to heal the wound, no matter how long it takes.

The Bible says that when we sow to the flesh, we reap from the flesh (Galatians 6:7-8). In other words, our actions have consequences. If you wounded your spouse, do not lecture about forgiveness. Instead, focus on healing the wound. Read Luke 19:8 for an example of a man who was willing to take giant steps to remedy past wrongs.

Pray for patience and concentrate on winning trust through your changed attitude and behavior. Jesus said,

"Blessed are the peacemakers" (Matthew 5:9). This is the time to be a peacemaker. Be ready to say during the coming months, "I understand your feelings and hope I can win back your trust" dozens or even hundreds of times.

Turn from sin.
Do not be content with simply feeling bad or wishing you could change. Make an action plan to overcome your problem and pray about it daily. Tell your spouse how you plan to avoid that sin in the future.

Walk humbly, but with your head held high.
Even if you must work long and hard to regain trust, even if your mate never forgives you, know that God forgives you. Although you have harmed your spouse and must minister to the pain you caused, be comforted by the love of God. Do not be cocky before your spouse because of God's forgiveness, but do not grovel.

Make it personal ___ 🖉

Do you need to win back your spouse's trust? If so, write your plan.

Do Not Constantly Ask Forgiveness

Most of us don't ask forgiveness often enough. Others, however, overdo it, apologizing for every little thing. If you do this, you may be insecure about your spouse's love. Perhaps you think that you are a bad person or that God does not like you. If so, you may have moved beyond humility into self-loathing.

If you constantly apologize, you demean the meaning of a true apology and run the risk of annoying your spouse.

You can escape insecurity about your spouse's love or God's love by more fully understanding who you are in Christ. Study Scriptures that illustrate God's love for you (1 John 3:1 and Ephesians 3:17-19), his forgiveness (Romans 8:1-2), and your purpose in him (Ephesians 2:10 and Romans 12:4-8).

Make it personal ____ 🖉

Do you apologize too much? ☐ Yes ☐ No

If so, what steps will you take to change this pattern?

Talk After Apologizing

Asking and granting forgiveness can lead to a conversation in which each gains a better understanding of the other. Skeeter and I have had some of our best talks in the aftermath of apologizing and forgiving. At these moments, we deeply experience our love and acceptance of each other. When we talk, we often look at the circumstances, what went wrong, and how to keep it from reoccurring. We strive to speak respectfully and understand one another. Both of us often apologize because in most cases we're both to blame to some degree.

If your mate does not want to talk after you apologize, do not try to force a conversation. Remember that your primary goal is to humble yourself, focus on changes you need to make, and let God work on your spouse.

Make it personal ___ 🖉

Do you and your spouse sometimes have good conversations after apologizing? ☐ Yes ☐ No

How do you think you could start such a conversation without getting into an argument?

Apply this Chapter to Yourself

You may have read this chapter thinking, "I wish my spouse would genuinely apologize for his or her sins against me." If so, read the chapter again with yourself in mind. Do *you* need to apologize more?

If your mate sins against you, do not become bitter because he or she doesn't apologize properly. Instead, read Chapter 5 on the art of forgiving.

Putting It All Together — Chapter 6

Key point: Ask forgiveness when you sin against your spouse. Do this even if you think that he or she is ninety-nine percent to blame.

Memory verse: *"If you . . . remember that your brother has something against you . . . go and be reconciled." (Matthew 5:23-24)*

Action plan: Choose one or two lessons from this chapter to work on this week:

1.

2.

My Plan

Now that you have finished reading this book, take a few minutes to review each chapter, particularly the "Putting It All Together" section at the end of each chapter. Choose from one to three things to work on in the coming month and write them on this page.

1.

2.

3.

Looking Ahead

Congratulations on making it to the end of the book! As you practice the principles you learned, you will see they provide a solid foundation for your marriage. Now it's time to build on that foundation.

In the next book in the "Marriage by the Book" series, *Making Christ the Cornerstone*, you will learn how to center your marriage in the Lord. There is nothing more important for your marriage. As Solomon wrote:

> *Unless the LORD builds the house, its builders labor in vain. Unless the LORD watches over the city, the watchmen stand guard in vain. (Psalm 127:1)*

In other words, if your marriage is not centered in the Lord, your efforts are in vain. This book will show you many down-to-earth ways to put this principle into practice.

May God richly bless your marriage as you continue to grow in the knowledge of his ways.

Guidelines for Small Group Leaders

Are you thinking about leading a small group study of *Laying a Solid Foundation*? If so, you likely are aware that something wonderful happens when people get together to study what God has to say.

If you are uncertain about leading a small group, let me reassure you. These pages describe a step-by-step action plan that will help you lead practical, Christ-centered studies.

This book is ideal for:

- Couples
- Individuals
- Small group studies
- Marriage classes
- Men's studies
- Women's studies
- Counseling, mentoring, and coaching

In the following pages, you will read:

- How to lead a great small group meeting
- How to structure a great small group meeting
- Six-week schedule with suggested discussion questions

How to Lead a Great Group Meeting

As a Christian educator and Marriage and Family Therapist for over twenty-five years, I have found these guidelines to be effective in creating successful small groups. However, every group is different. Feel free to adapt these guidelines to fit your group's needs.

Be an encourager.

Some people in your group may be going through hard times or desperately unhappy. Encourage everyone that God is able to do more than we can imagine (Ephesians 3:20).

Be an example in openness.

You are the leader, but you also are a group member. Let everyone know that you too are learning. Talk about some of your struggles and victories. When you are open, it encourages others to be open.

Generate group discussions.

Group members learn more when they actively participate instead of simply listening to you. Lead as a facilitator, not a teacher. Avoid talking too much. Instead, ask questions. Invite participation, but never pressure people to talk.

- Ask questions from the chapter you are studying.

- Create your own questions. The best questions for generating discussions can't be answered with "yes" or "no." For example: "What did you learn from this section? How can you apply this truth in your life?"

Guide discussions.

You are a facilitator, but also remember that you are the leader. Keep discussions on track.

However, be sensitive to the Holy Spirit. There may be times when it's important to deal with unrelated issues or questions. There also may be issues you can offer to discuss after the meeting.

If one member of your group levels an angry attack on another, gently intervene and show this person how to express feelings without hostility.

Encourage silent people to talk.

If someone rarely talks or is painfully shy, ask him or her an easy question. Another approach might be to ask the silent person ahead of time if it would be okay to ask him or her a specific question during the group discussion.

Encourage overly talkative people to listen.

It's not unusual for one person in a group to talk too much, making it difficult for others to share. If this happens, gently redirect the conversation to others. If you don't, the other members may feel bored or frustrated.

If your efforts to gently redirect conversations don't work, speak privately with the talkative person. Say that you appreciate his or her participation, but you want to encourage others to talk too. Ask for his or her help.

Emphasize personal application.

It's good to learn what the Bible says, but it's also important to put what we learn into practice. Invite group members to ask God to transform them and help them apply what they learn.

Get others involved in group leadership.

The more people are involved in a group, the more they feel committed to the group and to participating. Once you get started, ask people to help lead meetings or read passages. (Check with them privately ahead of time.) Also ask them to help in other ways such as preparing refreshments, leading icebreakers, and planning potlucks.

How to Structure a Great Meeting

Set the stage.

- Greet people warmly. Make them feel welcome.
- Consider offering snacks and beverages.
- Sit in a circle.

Follow a six-step meeting plan.

1. *Start with prayer.* Ask God to help each person be receptive to his truth and transformed by his Spirit.

2. *Have an icebreaker.* Ask everyone to answer a fun, easy question. Or invite each person to briefly share something that happened in his or her life the past week. (Once people talk in a group, it is easier for them to speak again.)

3. *Ask for stories (testimonies)* from people who practiced something they learned in the previous meeting.

4. *Review key points in the reading assignment.* (Optional: If your group is memorizing Bible verses, ask everyone to recite the memory verses.)

5. *Ask questions* to generate group discussions.

6. *Encourage everyone and close in prayer.* Consider asking people to pray for one another. Leave group members with a sense of hope and excitement that God will help them learn how to apply his Word.

Your first meeting

There's a lot of ground to cover the first time you get together. If possible, ask everyone to read the pages you will discuss before you meet.

If it is not possible to hand out books ahead of time, you could read key points in the first chapter at the meeting and then discuss them.

Or you could add one more meeting to your schedule. In your first meeting, you could get to know each other and wait until the next meeting to discuss the first chapter.

In addition to following the "six-step meeting plan," at the first meeting:

- **Introduce yourselves.**
  Ask everyone to introduce himself or herself.

- **Say that you, personally, are there to learn.**
  Let the group know you are not perfect, and that you are looking forward to learning together.

- **Go over "housekeeping" items such as:**

  - When the group will meet and how it will be structured

  - Ground rule of speaking respectfully

  - The importance of reading the chapter(s) and answering the "Make it personal" questions before meeting as a group.

  - Your confidentiality policy
    With few exceptions, what's said in the group stays in the group.

- **Ask group members for help.**
  Ask members of your group to help in ways such as preparing refreshments, leading icebreakers, and planning potlucks.

For more information

These suggestions are taken from my book *How to Lead a Christ-Centered Small Group*. To learn more about leading small groups, ask for it at your local bookstore, or order it online at www.DougBrittonBooks.com.

Week 1 Discussion Questions

Foreword, Introduction, Getting the Most, Chapter 1: Realize You Are "One Flesh"

In addition to the following questions, consider asking some "Make it personal" questions from this chapter.

What was the most helpful idea to you in "Getting the Most from this Book"?

What spoke to you the most in Chapter 1?

What does "one flesh" mean?

What is the difference between how most of the world looks at marriage and how God does?

What are some unrealistic expectations that people may bring into their marriage?

Did anyone check one or more boxes in "Common Reasons for Problems"?

What is one box you checked? Why?

Has any couple been an outstanding example to you of a great marriage? What can you learn from their example?

Can you think of a celebrity who is a bad example?

Why can we have hope, no matter how bad our marriage seems?

This chapter encourages us to look for the positive in our mate. Tell your spouse things that you appreciate or respect about him or her.

How will you apply what you learned in this meeting in the coming week? (Decide whether to invite people to share openly in the group or privately as a couple.)

Week 2 Discussion Questions

Chapter 2: Focus on Changes *You* Should Make

In addition to the following questions, consider asking some "Make it personal" questions from this chapter.

Why is it difficult to focus on yourself, not your spouse?

How many of you gave yourself a perfect score in "Evaluate Yourself by the Bible"?

Share with your spouse one of your low scores in "Evaluate Yourself by the Bible." Pray for help in that area. (Ask couples to talk privately. Those without spouses can speak with each other or with you.)

Have you ever seen two children get in a fight, each one blaming the other one for starting it? Do you think marital arguments often are like fights between two children?

What are Jesus' main points in Matthew 7:3-5?

Why is it important to take the plank out of our eye to be able to see clearly?

What are three questions you can ask yourself in a tense time? ("Did I contribute to the problem?" How can I help in this conversation?" How does God want me to speak?")

What can you do to remember these three questions?

Since Jesus said to first take the plank out of our own eye, does that mean we can't bring up frustrations?

How should we discuss our frustrations?

How will you apply what you learned in this meeting in the coming week? (Decide whether to invite people to share openly in the group or privately as a couple.)

Week 3 Discussion Questions

Chapter 3: Throw Yourself into Your Marriage

In addition to the following questions, consider asking some "Make it personal" questions from this chapter.

Why should we have to throw ourselves into our marriage? Shouldn't we just do what comes naturally?

Wouldn't it be phony to do something for your marriage if you don't feel like it?

In practical terms, how can you put your spouse before all others when you literally spend more time at work or with your children?

Almost everybody takes his or her mate for granted sometimes. How can we avoid falling into this trap?

Have you known someone who made the wrong sacrifices for his or her marriage that actually hurt their marriage?

How can you help with your children's homework and also make time for your spouse?

How does this chapter apply to couples who have children or elderly parents with special needs?

Have you thought your ministry is life-consuming and that your spouse should understand that?

Make a plan to do one marriage-building activity this week. (Ask couples to talk privately. Those without spouses can speak with each other or with you.)

How will you apply what you learned in this meeting in the coming week? (Decide whether to invite people to share openly in the group or privately as a couple.)

Week 4 Discussion Questions

Chapter 4: Commit to Your Marriage

In addition to the following questions, consider asking some "Make it personal" questions from this chapter.

How does God look at divorce? How important is this topic to him?

Does God look at marriage as a legal agreement, or as something deeper than that?

Why does God want people to get married instead of living together?

Why is commitment so important to marriage?

Did your parents divorce? What can you learn from their example?

Why should we never say, "Let's divorce"?

Would it ever be appropriate to separate, but not divorce?

If someone thinks he or she married the wrong person, or under the wrong circumstances, what should he or she do?

What should someone do if he or she stops feeling in love?

What are key ways to prevent divorce?

If someone has divorced for unscriptural reasons, what steps should he or she take?

How will you apply what you learned in this meeting in the coming week? (Decide whether to invite people to share openly in the group or privately as a couple.)

Week 5 Discussion Questions

Chapter 5: Forgive Your Spouse

In addition to the following questions, consider asking some "Make it personal" questions from this chapter.

What are some reasons it is so important to forgive?

Have you known someone who refused to forgive something? How did it affect him or her?

Have you known someone who forgave an awful thing? How did this affect him or her?

Are we supposed to only forgive big things? What about little things like neglecting to put the toothpaste away?

Does forgiving your spouse mean you can't talk about them?

If your mate apologizes but you don't think it's sincere, how should you respond?

My spouse keeps doing the same irritating thing. Do I have to keep forgiving?

How does forgiveness bring healing?

If you choose to forgive, but still feel upset, does that mean you haven't forgiven?

Is it possible to forgive someone yet still take strong actions?

Trust is important in marriage. Does that mean lying is unforgivable?

How will you apply what you learned in this meeting in the coming week? (Decide whether to invite people to share openly in the group or privately as a couple.)

Week 6 Discussion Questions

Chapter 6: Ask Forgiveness

In addition to the following questions, consider asking some "Make it personal" questions from this chapter.

Why is it important to follow up an apology by asking for forgiveness?

If your spouse starts an argument and you get angry, should you apologize for your anger?

What do you think about this apology: "I'm sorry for the way I talked when you pushed my buttons."

How should you respond if your spouse says he or she won't forgive you?

Should you apologize when your spouse also is at fault?

Jesus said, "Blessed are the peacemakers" in Matthew 5:9. Is asking forgiveness related to being a peacemaker?

Some people constantly apologize for every little thing. Why is that a bad idea?

If you did something wrong and your spouse continues to feel wounded after you apologize, what should you do?

Is it healthy to talk about a problem after apologizing?

Take turns asking forgiveness and granting forgiveness for anything that has not been forgiven yet. (Ask couples to talk privately. Those without spouses can speak with each other or with you.)

How will you apply what you learned in this meeting in the coming week? (Decide whether to invite people to share openly in the group or privately as a couple.)

More Resources

Books for Daily Living

These practical, Bible-based books by Doug Britton help readers apply God's truths in every area of life. They can be studied by individuals, couples, or groups.

Breaking Free from Alcohol and Drugs

Conquering Depression

Defeating Temptation

Healing Life's Hurts

How to Lead a Christ-Centered Small Group

Overcoming Jealousy and Insecurity

Strengthening Your Marriage

Successful Christian Parenting

Victory Over Grumpiness, Irritation, and Anger

Who Do You Think You Are?

Ask for these books at your local bookstore, or visit www.DougBrittonBooks.com.

Marriage by the Book

The truths in Doug Britton's eight-book "Marriage by the Book" series enrich strong marriages as well as strengthen hurting ones. These books can be studied as a series or as individual books. They are available with multi-ethnic or African-American covers.

Laying a Solid Foundation

Making Christ the Cornerstone

Encouraging Your Spouse

Extending Grace to Your Mate

Talking with Respect and Love

Improving Your Teamwork

Putting Money in its Place

Fanning the Flames of Romance

Marriage by the Book Group Leaders' Guide

Ask for these books at your local bookstore, or
visit www.DougBrittonBooks.com.

Books for Growing in Christ

(Discipleship Books)

These books by Doug Britton help readers understand the Bible and show how to grow as Jesus' disciples. They can be studied by individuals, couples, or groups.

Getting Connected

First Things First

Hand in Hand

Twenty-eight Days

Ask for these books at your local bookstore, or visit www.DougBrittonBooks.com.

About the Author

Doug Britton, MFT, has helped thousands of individuals and families as a Christian marriage and family therapist, seminar speaker, and co-host of a radio call-in show.

He also has trained hundreds of pastors, counselors, mentors, and lay leaders in biblical counseling, mentoring, and small group leadership.

In over twenty Bible-based books, Doug shares practical ways to apply God's Word to all areas of daily life.

Doug and his wife Skeeter live in Northern California.

Books: Doug has written books on many daily-living topics. Read about them at www.DougBrittonBooks.com.

Free online Bible studies for daily living: Read Doug's online studies on marriage, parenting, anger, self-concept, anxiety, depression, temptation, fear of death, biblical counseling, mentoring, small group leadership, and other topics. Visit www.DougBrittonBooks.com and click on the "Free online Bible studies" link.

Seminars and retreats: If you would like Doug or another member of the LifeTree Institute team to speak at a seminar in your church on any of the above topics, please visit www.DougBrittonBooks.com and click on the "Workshops" link.

Stay in Touch with Doug

Once or twice a month, Doug Britton sends brief email newsletters announcing:

- Free online Bible studies
- New books
- Seminars, workshops, and retreats

To receive Doug's email newsletters:

- Visit www.DougBrittonBooks.com
- Click on the "Email Newsletter" link